Unraveling the Mystery of

The Motivational Gifts

Your Gifts Discovery Manual

by

Rick Walston

PRESS

Unraveling the Mystery of The Motivational Gifts
by Rick Walston

Printed in the United States of America

Library of Congress Control Number: 2002112314
ISBN 1-591602-29-7

Xulon Press
11350 Random Hills Road
Suite 800
Fairfax, VA 22030
(703) 279-6511
XulonPress.com

To order additional copies, call 1-866-909-BOOK (2665).

Other books by Rick Walston

-*Walston's Guide to Christian Distance Learning Earning Degrees Nontraditionally* 4th Edition, 1999.

-*Walston's Guide To Earning Religious Degrees Non-Traditionally*, 3rd edition, 1997.

-*Walston's Guide To Earning Religious Degrees Non-Traditionally*, 2nd edition, 1994.

-*Walston & Bear's Guide To Earning Religious Degrees Non-Traditionally*, 1993.

-*Divorce and Remarriage: An Amplification of the Assemblies of God Position Paper on Divorce and Remarriage* (Gospel Publishing House, Springfield, MO., 1991).

Acknowledgments

Editing Helps and Comments

I wish to express my deep gratitude to Tyler Ramey, good friend and colleague, who spent many hours reading and editing and correcting the manuscript.

A special thanks goes to my student Carmen DiCello who also spent many hours reading and making suggestions. Also, my appreciation goes to my student Rob Myers who gave helpful feedback suggestions via the medium of email, and also I'd like to thank Dr. Larry Allen, Kevin Potts, and Luke Ahrens for their helpful suggestions.

Cover Art

Concerning the artwork for the cover of this book, I am deeply indebted to my good and long-time friend Cale Burr, B.A. (in Visual Communication, Western Washington University), artist *par excellence*. See Cale's Web Page at http://www.caleburr.com. His email address is cale@ caleburr.com.

Encouragement and Support

As always, I wish to thank the love of my life, my wife, Sue, for her constant encouragement and support.

Dedicated to Sue

About the Author

Dr. Walston is the founder and president of Columbia Evangelical Seminary, a distance learning school offering all levels of degrees through mentorship studies. For information about the seminary: www.columbia Seminary.edu. email: CES@tx3.net.

He has been researching, writing, and teaching on the subject of spiritual gifts since his own "gifts discovery" in 1982. He retired from pastoring after 20 years to dedicate himself full time to the ministry of Christian education.

Dr. Walston's educational background includes:
—*Doctor of Philosophy* in New Testament Theology, Potchefstroom University of South Africa
—*Doctor of Ministry*, Northwest Graduate School of the Ministry
—*Master of Religion*, Warner Pacific College
—*Bachelor of Arts*, Warner Pacific College
—*Associate of Practical Theology*, Christ for the Nations Institute

You can reach Dr. Walston at:
Columbia Evangelical Seminary
Attn: Dr. Rick Walston, President
P. O. Box 1189
Buckley, WA 98321
or, email him at: CES@tx3.net

Table of Contents

Chapter 1
  Unraveling the Mystery of the Motivational Gifts....17

Chapter 2
  Background to the Motivational Gifts 25

Chapter 3
  An Overview of the Motivational Gifts 33

Chapter 4
  Rose-Colored Glasses 49

Chapter 5
  Gift Projection 59

Chapter 6
  Some Characteristic Traits of the Seven
  Motivational Gifts 71

Chapter 7
  Biblical Personality Examples of the Seven
  Motivational Gifts..95

Chapter 8
  The Motivational Gifts in Ministry 117

Chapter 9
  Do Opposites Attract? A Prevailing Myth in
  Our Culture 135

Chapter 10
The Walston Gifts Indicator:
Determining Your Motivational Gifts 147

Appendix A
A Review of the Historical Development
of the Motivational Gifts Theory 167

Appendix B
A Brief Theology of Spiritual Gifts...........................187

Bibliography 213

Study Questions 221

Comments by some who attended Dr. Walston's Motivational Gifts Seminar or who read some of his writings on this topic.

The most liberating truth in my Christian life was discovering my Motivational Gift, and realizing that I had a purpose in God's ministry! Your book has been a great source of encouragement to me.

Your gifts seminar was just what my marriage needed. For the first time in years, we have begun to really communicate.

I have wondered for years what God's will for my life was concerning what aspect of ministry that I should be involved in. Now I know!

I always used to think that this theory of the "gifts" was completely without biblical warrant. Your teaching on this topic has shown me how wrong I was.

I have been a counselor for nearly 30 years, and I can see how this information will now enhance my counseling, especially with married couples.

I have only been a Christian for two years, and already I have discovered that God has gifted me to do His will. Thanks! This information has been as exciting as when I first got saved!

I have always wanted to be just like my pastor. Now, I want to be like Jesus. Maybe now that I have discovered my God-given gifts, I can begin to do that.

As a pastor who wants to see his people move into the various aspects of ministry that God has called them to, I thank you for this teaching on the Motivational Gifts. I plan to use your teachings on this topic in my church.

Chapter 1

Unraveling the Mystery of the Motivational Gifts

Introductory Information

I began researching the topic of Motivational Gifts in 1982 as a pastor. I discovered that there is a theory which identifies the gifts found in Romans 12:6-8 as being personality characteristics. Later, it began to dawn on me that these Motivational Gifts were synonymous in concept with psychological personality types.

Though many who attempt to teach on the motivational gifts have no clue that they are treading into psychology, the fact is they end up teaching that these gifts are personality types without even realizing it.

Important Point of Clarification

It is vitally important that people understand that the Motivational Gifts theory is not at odds with the traditional concept of the gifts of the Spirit. It merely attempts to identify the *personality types* of the people who have the gifts as listed in Romans 12: 6-8. For example, the concept of the *prophet* in this theory does not negate the traditional sense and understanding of the prophet (predictor and forthteller) found elsewhere in the Bible.

It is vitally important that people understand that the Motivational Gifts theory is not at odds with the traditional concept of the gifts of the Spirit.

This theory is not a study of the *function* of the Prophet (or Teacher or Exhorter, etc.), but of his or her *personality*. What kind of a person is he or she? Furthermore, the Motivational Gifts theory *does not* deny the function of the Prophet (or the other gifts) in the traditional sense.

Too many people have summarily rejected the Motivational Gifts theory because they misunderstood this fact. They thought that the Motivational Gifts theory was devised as an *alternative* to the traditional concept of the gifts. It wasn't. It attempts only to answer the question, "What are the personality types of the individuals with these particular gifts?"

Sadly, the reverse has happened as well. Some have accepted the Motivational Gifts theory and rejected the traditional way of viewing the gifts! But, again, this is not an "either-or" proposition.

The *traditional concept* of the prophet is *one who speaks on behalf of God* and sometimes may do so in a predictive mode. This traditional concept is not subverted by the Motivational Gifts theory. Rather, the Motivational Gifts theory simply attempts to identify *the prophet's personality*. What makes him or her tick?

So, let this be clear, the Motivational Gifts theory is *not* given as an *alternative* to the traditional concept of the functions of these gifts. It is given simply as a *complementary facet* of the gifts. A facet that we may not have considered before.

Motivational Gifts Theory

According to this theory, these particular gifts are

called Motivational Gifts because they depict one's *basic motivation* or *personality*. For example, the Motivational Gift of Prophecy in Romans 12:6 would be understood more as a personality type which is characteristic of a prophet, e.g., blunt, outspoken, and very determined concerning issues of morality. Likewise, the gift of *teaching* is not seen so much as the ability to teach nor as the ministry of teaching as in the Ephesians 4:11 sense. The gift of teaching is seen as a particular *personality type,* which is characteristic of a Teacher, e.g., logical and analytical. In a word, the Teacher is critically minded.

However, a person with the Motivational Gift of Teacher (Romans 12) may also be a Teacher in the Ephesians 4:11 category. Likewise, the Motivational Gift of Prophet may in fact fulfill the prophetic ministry and be an Ephesians 4:11 prophet.[1] But, one may have the Motivational Gift without being set in the ministry of the same.

The basis of this particular study of the gifts in Romans 12:6-8 is from theological, theoretical, and empirical evidence rather than strict exegesis. Also, there is no single, unified, large body of literature concerning this particular aspect of the gifts in Romans 12 to which one may refer. Therefore, there are not a lot of experts to turn to for help in developing this theory. There are, however, some disjointed statements by laymen, theologians, and psychologists which seem to support this particular theory of the Romans 12 list of gifts. By "disjointed" I mean that while there are statements that seem to provide a basis for the Motivational Gifts theory, the statements themselves are not part of a collective defense of the theory.

These various statements are also "disjointed" in the serendipitous nature of their discovery. I did not set out to locate statements for the defense of the Motivational Gifts theory. Rather, after having been introduced to the theory in the early 1980's, I was amazed at the amount of congruent statements I discovered in my every-day studies and research from then till now. This book is my effort to synthesize the various concepts into a collective whole.

Beyond the selective material from other writers and researchers, much of the material for this book is an expanded representation of my personal research. I am aware of only two authors who have written directly and openly on this theoretical position of the Motivational Gifts. However, both authors deal with these gifts on a less academic level than I do, and neither draws from psychological personality theory as do I.[2]

For the purposes of this book, I have accepted the theory that these particular gifts are to be understood as personality types. Because this is so, I have not overloaded the text with the word "theory." It is accepted and understood at the outset that this particular view of these gifts is, for the most part, theory.

Therefore, I will not seek to defend to any great extent this particular theory of the gifts. I will simply attempt to expound and accurately explain the theory. Geisler and Feinberg state that the scientific method of determining whether a statement (in this case a theory) is true has four steps: (1) explaining the statement or theory carefully and clearly; (2) predicting the outcomes of such a theory or belief; (3) performing controlled experiments to confirm or refute the predicted outcomes and observing the results; and (4) accepting or rejecting the final results.[3] Though I do not point out when I use these four steps of determining truth, I have incorporated each of them into this research.

The *empirical* evidence indicates that this theory is helpful to many of God's people. Many Christians have been introduced to the theory of Motivational Gifts. Some writers, while not having written books about it, have also taught on these gifts. Speaking of this particular theory of the gifts in Romans 12, Bill Gothard says that the Motivational Gifts theory and implementation has helped thousands of Christians discover and use their spiritual gifts.[4]

I have also had various opportunities to teach this material to several hundreds of people in different settings (both in and outside the church) over the last decade. Like Gothard, I can report that it has had a positive effect upon those who heard and participated in the material. However, positive experiences notwithstanding, experience alone is not the verification of truth. Geisler and Feinberg have accurately explained that an experience only proves that one has had an experience.[5]

Yet, on the other hand, not all truth learned through experience is necessarily suspect just because it has come from experience. Geisler and Feinberg also state that it is wrong to insist that there is only one method by which we can discover truth.[6]

In the final analysis, my goal is to expound the Motivational Gifts *theory* and to support it by theology, Scripture, experience, and logic. I will leave it to my readers to determine if I succeeded.

---

[1] It is not within the scope of this research to discuss the perpetuity of the gifts and their limitations today in contradistinction to the New Testament days. Suffice it to say that I believe that there are still Ephesians 4:11 prophets today, but they are not "foundational prophets" as were the prophets of the New Testament era.

[2] The authors are Bill Gothard, *How To Understand Spiritual Gifts* (Oak Brook, Il.: Institute in Basic Life Principles, 1981), and Don and Katie Fortune, (counted as one author because of their joint authorship of two volumes) *Discover Your God-Given Gifts* (Old Tappan, N.J.: Fleming H. Revell Company, 1987), and *Discover Your Children's Gifts* (Old Tappan, N.J.: Fleming H. Revell Company, 1989).

[3] Norman A. Geisler and Paul D. Feinberg, *Introduction to Philosophy* (Grand Rapids, Mi.: Baker Book House, 1980), p. 63.

[4] Gothard, *How To Understand*, p. 49.

[5] Geisler and Feinberg., p. 51.

[6] Ibid., 52.

Chapter 2

Background to the Motivational Gifts

The first and primary thing that you must know and believe about spiritual gifts is that you have one. You may not even realize it, but you operate in your gift every day.

Many who read this book may end up feeling a sense of discovery of who they are and why they perceive things the way they do. By reading this book, many will discover their spiritual gifts, and they will learn how to move forward in the ministry that God has entrusted to them. Certainly, not everyone is called to full-time Christian ministry, but all Christians have ministries that God has called them to. Does that sound contradictory? It shouldn't. God has called every believer to be involved in ministry; however, not all Christians are to be full-time pastors, full-time Christian professors, full-time evangelists, etc. Yet, God wants to use every member of the body of Christ in some aspect of personal ministry. And, to that end, He has equipped each member of the Body of Christ with a special ability to do what it is He wants them to do. This "special ability" is called a *spiritual gift*.

When some people think of spiritual gifts, they think only of those listed in 1 Corinthians 12. Of course many get confused when they look at those gifts in 1 Corinthians 12. They see the gifts of the *Workings of Miracles* or the *Gifts of Healings*, but they don't see anything that fantastic and wonderful happening in their own lives. And, what about that mysterious but wonderful sounding gift called the *Word of Wisdom*? Wouldn't it be great to have that one? Or, how about the *Word of Knowledge*? As we take this journey of unraveling the mystery gifts together, I will help you—step by step—make sense of it all.

The next thing that we must understand is that 1 Corinthians 12 is not the only list of gifts in the Bible. There are three *primary* lists of gifts, and there are different ways of understanding how they function. Some people will disagree with the way I categorize and explain them, and that's quite all right. Even if you do not completely agree with my perspective, I think you will gain a much better understanding of the gifts overall. For others, however, I believe that this book will be an eye-opening journey. Come then, as we *unravel the mystery of the spiritual gifts.*

The Word "Gift" Defined

In brief, a spiritual gift is a grace-gift from God. It bestows a special spiritual ability upon a member of the Body of Christ to equip that person to fulfill the will of God and edify the other members of the Body.

Unraveling the Categories

The basic passages of Scripture that are pertinent to the understanding of spiritual gifts are Ephesians 4:1-16, 1 Corinthians 12-14, Romans 12:1-9, 1 Peter 4:7-11, 1 Timothy 4:11-16, and 2 Timothy 1:3-14. Obviously this list is not all inclusive, but it reflects some of the major portions that are relevant to this study. However, to make things very simple, and because there is gift-overlap among these lists, it is perhaps best to review only three major lists and to categorize them. These three main categories of spiritual gifts are:

1. *Ministry Gifts (Ephesians 4)*
2. *Manifestations of the Spirit (1 Corinthians 12)*
3. *Motivational Gifts (Romans 12)*

This book will be primarily interested in the third category of gifts, i.e., the Motivational Gifts found in Romans 12. Later, you will actually discover (through the *Walston Gifts Indicator,* WGI[1]) which gifts of the Romans 12 list you have. However, before we can look at the Romans 12 list of gifts, we must review the three categories and understand each gift in each list. By the time we arrive at the primary subject of our study—the Romans 12 Motivational Gifts—you should have a good basic understanding of the differences among these three categories.

Psychological Theory of Personality Types

There is a well-known theory in psychology called *Personality Types.* It states that different people have different personalities. This is so basic to human understanding that the idea that it takes a trained psychologist or psychiatrist to tell us this is quite nearly silly. Any parent who has raised children knows that there are different personalities and temperaments among their children. Likewise, pastors do not need to be told that people have differing personalities. That people have differing personalities is as obvious as the fact that people come in different shapes and sizes.

Two of the most commonly identified personality types are those of shyness and outgoingness. Grade-school teachers are constantly attempting to calm the gregarious children and inspire the shy ones to some outward action or social interaction. So, the fact is no one seriously doubts that humans have differing personalities and character traits.

Do we really believe that God is the author (creator) of our personalities? I do. And, I contend that we can see these personalities in the gifts that God has given to us. However, the details of the different personalities and of the methods used to determine the more subtle differences in personality types are not as obvious. While it may be obvious to a school teacher who clearly sees that "Gregarious Gail" is outgoing and a bit obnoxious and that "Introvert Ivan" is shy and a loner, it is less obvious to the teacher that there are differences between "Gregarious Gail" and "Extrovert Ellen." On the face of it, Gail and Ellen may appear quite similar. However, when certain things transpire in class or on the playground, Gail and Ellen may in fact respond differently to these same events.

Whereas they are both extroverts, there are differences between Gregarious Gail and Extrovert Ellen. One girl might "process" information rationally (in a logical, empirical way) whereas the other might "process" that same information intuitively. Thus, there is a subtle distinction between these two extrovert girls. Furthermore, Gail and Ellen may "process" their decisions based on differing psychological distinctions.

Gail makes her decisions and actions based upon what she thinks is right or wrong, good or bad, with little or no thought of the *emotional* impact that her actions (or words) have upon herself or others. Ellen, however, makes her decisions and actions based precisely upon what she thinks will be the *emotional* impact that her actions (or words) have upon herself or others. In a word, Gail acts from logic and Ellen acts from emotion. As these differences, called "preferences" in psychology, are observed and classified in each person, an individual, personal, personality type emerges.

Psychology and Theology?

Many Bible-believing Christians are understandably wary of psychology. However, this *particular theory of the gifts*, i.e., Motivational Gifts, blends quite well with *some of the truths* discovered through the psychological research of personality types. I agree with Christian philosophers Norman Geisler and Paul Feinberg that *all truth is God's truth.*[2] If a reality (truth) is discovered by means other than direct biblical research, it is God's truth anyway. All truth is God's truth whether discovered in the NASA Jet Propulsion Laboratory, in the medical laboratory, in psychological research, or in theological study.

All truth is God's truth whether discovered in the NASA Jet Propulsion Laboratory, in the medical laboratory, in psychological research, or in theological study.

I am certainly not trying to validate all psychology nor harmonize all psychology with theology (a project doomed to failure). The use of psychology in this research and writing is limited and focused and has to do with only that personality theory which is typically referred to as Psychological Type. Furthermore, it is also somewhat limited to Isabel Briggs Myers' research and interpretation of Carl Jung's theory of psychological types.[3]

Much of the truth about psychological types is harmonious with the Motivational Gifts theory. Just as there are various psychological (personality) types, so there are differing gifts which in essence make up differing personality types. Gary Harbaugh, a Christian psychologist agrees that it is possible "to integrate psychological insight with theological understanding."[4] Further, Harbaugh sees—as I do—human personalities as gifts from God.[5]

---

[1] The gifts indicator in chapter 10 is called the *Walston Gifts Indicator* and shall also be referred to as the WGI.

[2] Norman A. Geisler and Paul D. Feinberg, *Introduction to Philosophy* (Grand Rapids, Mi.: Baker Book House, 1980), p. 22.

[3] I am aware of some of the obviously strange and non-Christian things that Carl Jung believed and taught. Thus, I am certainly not attempting to "blend" all of *Jung's* psychology with Christian theology or the Motivational Gifts theory.

[4] Gary L. Harbaugh, *God's Gifted People* (Minneapolis, Mn.: Augsburg Publishing House, 1988), p. 20.

[5] Ibid., p. 17.

Chapter 3

An Overview of the Motivational Gifts

There are seven Motivational Gifts. In biblical order they are Prophet, Server, Teacher, Exhorter, Giver, Administrator, and Mercy. It is the position of the Motivational Gifts Theory that these gifts are the various personalities that God has given to different individuals.

The People of the Gifts

Throughout this book, the Motivational Gifts are listed and discussed as nouns rather than verbs. For instance, when Romans 12:7 says "he who teaches, in his teaching," the emphasis will be more on the noun *he* (the Teacher) of the verse than upon the verbs *teaches* or *teaching*. In fact, this particular Motivational Gift is not the act of teaching *per se.* Therefore, one may have the gift of Teacher and never actually teach in a classroom. Just the same, a person with the Motivational Gift of Prophet is not necessarily a prophet in the Ephesians 4:11 sense, nor will that person necessarily function in the gift of prophecy as listed in 1 Corinthians 12:10. However, though the "Teacher" may never teach and the "Prophet" may never prophesy, it is more likely that they will—if given the opportunities—operate in the ministry forms of their gifts. The biblical text that lists the Motivational Gifts is Romans 12:6-8. However, the first five verses of chapter twelve set the contextual stage for the listing of the gifts. Romans 12:1-8 is reproduced below:

I urge you therefore, brethren, by the mercies of

God, to present your bodies a living and holy sacrifice, acceptable to God, which is your spiritual service of worship. And do not be conformed to this world, but be transformed by the renewing of your mind, that you may prove what the will of God is, that which is good and acceptable and perfect. For through the grace given to me I say to every man among you not to think more highly of himself than he ought to think; but to think so as to have sound judgment, as God has allotted to each a measure of faith. For just as we have many members in one body and all the members do not have the same function, so we, who are many, are one body in Christ, and individually members one of another. And since we have gifts that differ according to the grace given to us, let each exercise them accordingly: if *prophecy*, according to the proportion of his faith; if *service*, in his serving; or he who *teaches*, in his teaching; or he who *exhorts*, in his exhortation; he who *gives*, with liberality; he who *leads*, with diligence; he who shows *mercy*, with cheerfulness (emphasis added).[1]

The Will of God

It appears from the context of Romans 12:1-8 that these spiritual gifts are correlated with the will of God. Paul makes it clear that each Christian is a special part or member of the Body of Christ (verses 4-5). Each member of the human body has a particular function or functions; for example, the ears hear, the nose smells, the fingers feel and grasp, and no member needs to be taught what its basic function is. The members are in the will of the head by functioning in their *natural capacity.*

It appears from the context of Romans 12:1-8 that these spiritual gifts are correlated with the will of God.

Even though the fingers and hands feel and grasp as *natural exercises* of who and what they are, it takes training for those same hands to perform a delicate task, like playing a musical instrument for example. Likewise, a Romans 12 Prophet or Teacher, and the others listed there, must be trained in their natural functions so as to be more sophisticated and mature in their operations. Have you ever heard children playing instruments in orchestras? Often, the sound they make is more noise than music. Yet, with practice they get better. When they are finally capable of playing their instruments in harmony with the other members of the orchestra, their hands are able to perform the joyous task of making beautiful music. So it is with the joyful task of exercising spiritual gifts.

People who are just beginning to function in their areas of giftedness may at first make many mistakes and they may even become discouraged. However, given the proper opportunities and the correct training, they can begin to find and function in their particular God-given place in His "orchestra."

People Types and Tiger Stripes[2]

When members of the Body of Christ discover their particular gifts, they will subsequently function in the natural exercise of their giftedness (position), and thus fulfill, as a natural outcome, the will of their head who is Christ. When people have a correct perspective of themselves (Rom 12:3) and their ministries, it follows that, in a general sense, they will naturally and automatically know the will of God for their lives. For, just as the eyes naturally "know" that the will of the head is for them to function in the "ministry of sight," and the ears naturally "know" that the will of the head is for them to function in the "ministry of hearing," so the gifted Giver knows *naturally* (perhaps not even consciously) that it is the will of the Head (Christ) for him to function in the ministry of giving. The person gifted with the Motivation of Mercy knows *naturally* to show or demonstrate mercy to fellow humans. The will of God is fulfilled in the Mercy individual by his or her demonstration of mercy.

Pastor Daniel Brown explains it by suggesting that the spice cinnamon doesn't have to do something to be cinnamon; it just is what it is. Light too, does not have to perform its act of lighting things; when it comes into contact with objects, its *nature* is to illuminate them.[3] Cinnamon and light have properties or characteristics that are the essence of what they are. They don't have to perform to be what they are; they just are. Likewise, each person has a primary characteristic or property (giftedness), which is the essence of who he or she is. When that property is discovered and released, e.g., mercy, administration, exhortation, etc., then the person is being naturally what he or she was created *to be* (not necessarily *to do*).

It further appears that when Christians know and operate in their particular gifts, they will not think more highly or lowly of themselves than they ought to, and they will have sound judgments of themselves according to the measure of faith (or giftedness) which God has bestowed upon them. Romans 12:3 speaks of this: "For by the grace given me I say to every one of you: Do not think of yourself more highly than you ought, but rather think of yourself with sober judgment, in accordance with the measure of faith God has given you." It is within *this context* that the Motivational Gifts are listed. To have a knowledge of your giftedness allows you to understand and develop those inherent properties that God has placed in you so that in so *being,* you *will do* the will of God. Thus, being precedes doing.

In short, to know one's gift is to know naturally or inherently, in a general sense, the will of God for one's life. The particulars of God's will, e.g., when, where, and with whom you should minister the grace of God, may not be automatically known by discovering your area of giftedness. But the what, i.e., *what it is,* that you are to do in fulfilling your ministry, for example, teach, administrate, exhort, etc., is known. The natural outcome of knowing who (or what) you are, is to know what you are to do. Searching and knowing God's will involves service for God by properly evaluating your gifts and exercising those gifts in the Body of Christ.

In the book *People Types and Tiger Stripes*, a

psychological text on personality theory, Gordon Lawrence answers the question: "How does a person get to be a type?" This is the same issue that Daniel Brown addressed above. Lawrence's answer is brief and cogent. He says that one becomes a *type* by doing what comes naturally.[4] Even the title of Lawrence's book suggests that personality types are as natural and inherent as the stripes on a tiger. Thus, Daniel Brown is correct in saying that we find what we are to do by finding what we are, and Gordon Lawrence agrees by implying that personality types are as natural and inherent as the stripes on a tiger, and that we get to be a type by doing what comes naturally. For example, I do not have to teach to be a Teacher in the Motivational Gifts sense; I just am what I am, i.e., a Teacher. However, it is good when I discover my gift and use it for the edification of the body of Christ. But, sadly, many people haven't a clue as to their giftedness or personality type. So, the fact remains that we all need to discover (or *uncover*) what our type (Motivational Gift) is.

The Charismata

The scriptural term for these gifts is *grace gifts*. Romans 12:6 says, "We have gifts that differ according to the grace given to us." The word *gifts* in this verse is from the Greek word *charismata* and they are given by the grace of God. The *charismata* (plural) are God's *enablements* given to Christians by the power and operation of the Holy Spirit. Thus, an accurate paraphrase of this verse could say: "We have been given special enablements by the grace of God to perform the ministry to which He has called us"

(Romans 12:6). Using again the human body as an illustration, the point of this verse can also be made clear in this paraphrase: "The Head has graciously given the eyes the enablement of sight to be equipped for the ministry of seeing, to which the Head has called them." The enablements Paul speaks of are the Motivational Gifts of Prophet, Server, Teacher, Exhorter, Giver, Administrator, and Mercy. And, you may be a Prophet, a Server, a Teacher, an Exhorter, a Giver, an Administrator, or a Mercy. It will be our job together in this book to help you discover which one you are.

These enablements are given by the gracious hand of God. No one worked for or earned a Motivational Gift. God has freely (by His grace) bestowed a Motivational Gift upon each person. Your Motivational Gift is God's gift to you, and your gift to God is what you accomplish through the exercise of your gift.

Further, these Motivational Gifts are not simply natural talents to be dedicated to God. Since the Giver is divine, the gifts are of supernatural origin. When you exercise your God-given Motivational Gift in the will of God for the edifying of the Body of Christ, the exercise of that gift is energized by the power of the Holy Spirit "according to the grace given us" (Romans 12:6). For instance, when Givers give to needy people as an exercise of their Motivational Gift, it is not a natural ability through which they respond. For natural, fallen humans are not generous but selfish, self-indulgent, and self-serving.

However, the *exercise* of these various gifts may be less than divine when used outside the will of God for something other than the edification of the Body of Christ. The gifts of God can be abused and misused. This is done in much the same way as those who have exercised the more spectacular gifts and yet will not be admitted into heaven (Matthew 7:21 ff.).

The Term Motivational

The term "Motivational" is not a scriptural term, but it is an accurate one for the *function* of these gifts because they are the *motivating factors* in every person.

The very thing that motivates one to view a situation in a certain way or to react a certain way to a given situation can be identified as one of these basic seven Motivational Gifts. For instance, several people may choose to give money to Christian organizations from differing motivations. Those with the Motivational Gift of Mercy may be motivated to give to organizations that help starving children, or they may give aid to a relief fund for disaster victims. The Mercy-gifted people are motivated to help those in distress, and they want their money to go to help such people. Those with the Motivational Gift of Prophet may be moved to give financial help to organizations that are preaching the "unadulterated Word of God." The "Prophet" is motivated to help the Word of the Lord get out to a spiritually lost and dying world. Those with the Motivational Gift of Teacher may desire to give financial assistance to organizations that are teaching and training people for the ministry. The "Teacher" is motivated to help promulgate the teaching of the Word of God. Thus, if you can accurately discover what it is that motivates you, you will be much closer to discovering which of the seven Motivational Gifts God has placed in you and which constitutes your particular personality.

Personality Filters

The term "Personality Filters" is also descriptive of the Motivational Gifts. All human communication is filtered through the personalities of both the speaker and the hearer (or writer and reader). Whatever it is that one is trying to express will be filtered (and thereby influenced) by his or her particular personality.

All human communication is filtered through the personalities of both the speaker and the hearer.

Thus, if a person has a sweet and merciful personality type, e.g., Motivational Gift of Mercy (or psychological preference of Feeling), then whatever that person communicates will be filtered or "screened" through that sweet and merciful personality. Every person has a Personality Filter through which communication travels, and the words spoken or attitudes expressed are filtered through that person's Personality Filter. When people identify their particular Personality Filter, i.e., Motivational Gift, they will understand how their particular gift affects the communication that they attempt to express.

Everyone has had the experience of meeting someone for the first time and there seems to be an immediate bonding of personalities. One may come away from meeting such a person saying, "That's my kind of man," or

"She thinks a lot like me." The reason for the immediate rapport may be that both parties have the same, or nearly the same, Personality Filter. On the other hand, people have also experienced just the opposite as well. Two people meet, and there seems to be an immediate disagreement about nearly everything. One may come away from such a meeting saying, "I surely wouldn't want that person on *my* team," or "We have a definite personality conflict," or, even, "We just don't see eye to eye." Most likely, these two do not have the same Personality Filter or there would not be such an immediate clash.

One of the greatest keys to working as a "team" is to know your own Personality Filter (Motivational Gift) and those of your coworkers. When you know what the other person's Personality Filter is, you can better understand why he or she sees and does things the way that he or she does. The knowledge that one's coworker sees things differently because of his or her particular Personality Filter and not simply because of ignorance (or worse, obstinacy) helps enhance interpersonal communication. Then, different perspectives can be expressed and appreciated for their particular contribution. Sometimes a combination of various perspectives is exactly what is needed to resolve a problem or to achieve a goal.

The "Personality Filter" and "Motivational Gift" are the same thing. The difference is not the element but the effect. If your Motivational Gift is Mercy, you will be *motivated* by the attitude of mercy. Since your Motivational Gift is Mercy, your Personality Filter will be mercy. Therefore, you will be motivated by mercy, and your speech and actions will be *filtered* through, or influenced by, mercy. Your Motivational Gift is the very essence of your personality. Simply put, the Motivational Gift identifies and filters who and what you are, and how you appear to others.

A Primary Motivational Gift

In much the same way as in psychological type theory, each believer will have only one, that is one *primary*, Motivational Gift. It must be thoroughly emphasized that everyone will have a primary spiritual gift. Spiritual gifts are for all believers. Often those who are not in formal ministry do not know, and some do not believe, that they have a spiritual gift. In virtually every area of your daily activities, you make decisions and live life according to your primary giftedness. First Peter 4:10 says, "As each one has received a special gift, employ it in serving one another, as good stewards of the manifold grace of God" (NASB). Thus, each believer has *a* special gift.

Distinguishing Primary and Auxiliary Gifts

Also in much the same way as in psychological type theory, it is not uncommon for people to struggle at differentiating their gifts. A person may have a strong auxiliary gift and thus not be sure which of the two (i.e., primary and auxiliary) gifts should fall into which category. Some who attempt to discover their gifts will ask a question of themselves such as, "Am I a prophet-teacher or a teacher-prophet?" In some instances a person will find it difficult to distinguish the primary gift from the auxiliary gift. What may compound this difficulty is that most people do not identify with all of the characteristics of a given gift. In fact, a person is not expected to identify with every last trait within a Motivational Gift description. Thus, sometimes people struggle to determine their primary gift from their auxiliary gift. When this happens, they must first have a good knowledge of the different characteristics of the two gifts. Also, they must conscientiously be aware of the choices and responses they make in their daily living, and they must categorize those decisions and responses. In some cases, *only after a careful categorization* of your actions, thoughts, ideas, responses, and choices throughout a week or two or even a month (sometimes more) will you be confidently able to identify your primary Motivational Gift from your auxiliary Motivational Gift.

On the other hand, some people have a strong primary gift which is obvious and distinct from their auxiliary gift. For instance, some may have the primary Motivational Gift of Teacher. Thus, they will be very logical and analytical. However, they may also have the *auxiliary gift* of Prophet. Thus, they will also see the world from a very moral and ethical perspective. When they logically consider the traits of the gift of Teacher, they will see themselves very clearly in most (if not all) of the Teacher's traits. They will also identify with certain characteristics of the Prophet, though not as many as with the Teacher. Thus, they may see their "reflection" in more than one gift. Generally, however, this "reflection" will be *more apparent* in one particular Motivation than any other.

Some mature believers find it difficult to identify their primary gift because they identify with many characteristics of several gifts. I have a theory that some older persons who have grown and matured in both the grace of God and in natural social graces may find it more difficult to identify their primary gift. The reason is that people who have been exposed to many different situations throughout their lives may have learned to exercise the various gifts of God when the needs arise. Over a lifetime of varied situations, flexible responses, and maturity, a person may actually become proficient in the exercise of several gifts. For instance, a person who does not have the gift of Mercy as one of her three highest gifts may learn how to administer mercy. If, for example, she actively takes care of the less-fortunate for many years as part of her occupational vocation, she may develop the ability to minister mercy even though her primary (first), auxiliary (second), and tertiary (third) gifts do not include Mercy. However, a lack of empirical data keeps this theory speculative.[5]

Each person will have one primary gift. However, in many instances people will also have a strong auxiliary gift and in some cases even a strong tertiary gift. I have formed an acronym from the initial letters of the three highest gifts. Using the first letter of each of the words, Primary, Auxiliary, and Tertiary (PAT), I call the three highest gifts one's PAT-Mix. For example, one's PAT-Mix may be Teacher, Prophet, and Exhorter, or perhaps Administrator, Giver, and Mercy. Some people may not have a PAT-Mix at all because they may function most of the time in only one gift, while the other gifts are rarely or seldom used.

Summary

The seven Motivational Gifts are Prophet, Server, Teacher, Exhorter, Giver, Administrator, and Mercy. These Motivational Gifts are personality types that God has given to different individuals.

Much can be learned from the study of psychological types. Also, some portions of personality theory are harmonious with the Motivational-Gifts theory.

The emphasis of the Motivational-Gifts theory is upon the personality types of the gifts rather than on the action of the gifts. Thus, this book is interested in the person of the Motivational Gifts, not, necessarily, the act of the ministry of the gifts.

To know your own Motivational Gift is to know, in a general sense, God's will for your ministry. Just as the members of a human body have particular functions, so also the members of the Body of Christ have their particular functions. Christians functioning in the natural exercise of their gifts will fulfill, in part, the will of God for their lives.

The Motivational Gifts are free gifts of God. In fact, since the word "gift" means something transferred without compensation, the expression "free gift" is redundant. However, for clarification, I call these *free gifts*. No one worked for or earned his or her Motivational Gift.

The term "Motivational" is an accurate term describing the function of these gifts. For, they are the motivating factors in the human psyche.

The Motivational Gifts can also properly be called "Personality Filters." Communication is filtered through one's Personality Filter. Personality Filters and Motivational

Gifts are the same thing. The difference is in the effect not the element.

Each person will have only one primary Motivational Gift. However, some may have a strong auxiliary gift, and some may even have a strong tertiary gift.

---

[1] Scripture taken from the *Holy Bible, New International Version,* © 1973, 1984 (unless otherwise noted). International Bible Society. Used by permission of Zondervan Bible Publishers.

[2] This delightful title was taken from a book by the same name: Gordon Lawrence, *People Types and Tiger Stripes*, 2nd ed. (Gainesville, Fl.: Center for Applications of Psychological Types, 1987).

[3] Daniel A. Brown, "Fashioned for Significance," *Spiritual Gift-Mixes* (Aptos, Ca.: The Coastlands, 1993-1994), lecture 1 of 11 on cassette.

[4] Gordon Lawrence, *People Types and Tiger Stripes*, 2nd ed. (Gainesville, Fl.: Center for Applications of Psychological Types, 1987), p. 18.

[5] There were some older and well-adjusted individuals who participated in the *Walston Gifts Indicator* who in fact did find it difficult to identify their primary gifts because they identified with many of them. However, my lack of knowledge concerning their backgrounds and maturity levels, and the small number of such individuals in my research made it impossible for me to draw any solid conclusions.

Chapter 4

Rose-Colored Glasses

Not only are the Motivational Gifts the motivating factors (and Filters) in each person's inner being, they can also be seen as the "rose-colored glasses" through which people see their world.

Let me demonstrate this with the Motivation of Mercy for example:

Mercy is the Motivational Gift and personality type that a particular person has. Thus, this person will be a "nice" person who is warm and friendly to others.

Information Input (received) Mercy is the "lens" (Rose Colored Glasses, or perception) through which this person sees the world. Thus, this Mercy-Person will "take in" and "assess" any outside stimuli (information) from the perspective of mercy.

Information Output (conveyed) Mercy is also the Filter through which the information will be conveyed or transmitted to others. When the Mercy-Person shares information with others, he/she will filter it through the Mercy *grid* so as to make it more palatable to those receiving the information.

As you can imagine, we could do this with all of the remaining Motivational Gifts. Each person receives and perceives information via his/her particular "colored-glasses" (i.e., perspective) and then each will process that information through a particular personality type. Then, each will convey that information to others through his/her particular *filter*, which filters the information to reflect a particular personality type. This is precisely why two or more people can witness the same event or listen to the same lecture and yet come away with varying perspectives on the event or lecture and also convey that information to others in sometimes considerably different ways. I have attempted to illustrate this reality of "colored-glasses" and filters below. I have given various likely responses of individuals to the same hypothetical situation.

Various Perspectives

In this hypothetical situation, a Christian brother in the church has lost his job. Each of the seven Motivational Gifts is represented. Upon hearing of the brother's misfortune, the variously gifted people respond uniquely from their particular perspectives and see this situation through their particular "colored glasses." Some possible responses of the seven Motivations to this situation are listed below. (As you read through these various responses, see if you identify with any of them.)

The Prophet's Perspective

The Prophet may come to this brother and say something like: *"God has a purpose for everything; so what is it that God is trying to show you through losing your job? Maybe you lost your job because there is sin in your heart."* The Prophet in this situation seems motivated to correct the supposed underlying ethical and moral problem.

The Server's Perspective

The Server may say something like: *"I bought you a*

newspaper so we could look for a job for you. If you need me to, I will drive you around to check on different prospects." The Server is motivated to meet the physical needs.

The Teacher's Perspective

The Teacher may say something like: *"Do you know exactly why you lost your job? I mean, was it something you did or didn't do? Did anyone else lose his job?"* The Teacher is motivated to get the facts and help the person arrive at a logical conclusion as to why he lost his job.

The Exhorter's Perspective

The Exhorter may say something like: *"Next time you will know better what to do, or not do, so you can avoid losing your job. But don't be too upset about all of this, after all, God is going to teach you something from it."* The Exhorter is motivated to get the person to grow from the experience and to look to the future.

The Giver's Perspective

The Giver may say something like: *"Here are some groceries you are going to need, and here is some money for gas for your car. If you need anything else while you are off work, let me know, and I will help you."* The Giver is motivated to meet the financial and material needs.

The *Administrator's* Perspective

The Administrator may say something like: *"I have made a list of all the job prospects available. So let's go through them to see which one is the best for you."* The Administrator is motivated to help the person reach a goal.

The *Mercy's* Perspective

Mercy may say something like: *"I was so saddened to hear that you lost your job. I'm sure this must be a real emotional stress on you at this time. But do not worry too much; I'm sure everything will work out. I will be praying for you."* Mercy is motivated to relieve any type of emotional or mental stress caused by the job loss.

These responses are oversimplified to be sure, but they give us an idea of how each person, with differing motivations, views situations from his or her own unique perspective.

Operate in *All* the *Gifts*

There is sometimes a danger in finding one's particular gift, or recognizing which set of "colored glasses" one primarily looks through. The danger is thinking that since each person has only one *primary* Motivational Gift, one is not required to operate in any of the other Motivations. But Scripture plainly teaches that no matter what Motivational Gift one possesses, one is still charged by God to function in the other gifts as well.

The fact that each person has only one *primary* Gift leads to the conclusion that each person will perceive through his or her primary Gift. Also, each person will operate more from that primary perspective than any other gift or perspective. Thus, the person *prefers* the primary Motivation over the others, but he or she is not to exclude the others.

This is true in much the same way that right-handed people *prefer* to do more difficult tasks that require greater manual dexterity and skill with their right hands. However, right-handed preferences notwithstanding, right-handed people also use their left hands constantly. Likewise, gifted people will not operate *only* in their primary gifts, seeing *solely* through one set of "colored glasses," but they will, almost constantly, operate in their auxiliary and tertiary gifts as well. Furthermore, Christians *are to operate in all of the gifts* when it is necessary and appropriate to do so.

Of Roles and Gifts

There is a distinction to be made between what may be called a "role" (function) and a "gift." For example, the person with the Motivational Gift of Prophet may at times, when the need arises, fulfill the role, or function, of mercy. As an example, all Christians are called to fulfill their role as a witness for Christ. In Acts, Jesus told his disciples, and by extension all Christians throughout all ages, "But you will receive power when the Holy Spirit comes on you; and you will be my witnesses in

There is a distinction to be made between what may be called a "role" and a "gift."

Jerusalem, and in all Judea and Samaria, and to the ends of the earth" (Acts 1:8). In that He said that Christians were to witness of Him "to the ends of the earth," He included all Christians in all history. Thus, all Christians are responsible to fulfill the role of a witness. However, there is a special gift of evangelist that is not given to every person in the body of Christ (Ephesians 4:11). This gift of evangelist is not a role, it is a gift; and while all are called to the role of witnessing, only some are called to be evangelists. Likewise, the Motivational Gifts must not be confused with their role counterparts. Thus, Christians should not say that they shall never operate in any of the other gifts beyond their primary Motivations. For *all* are called to function in *all* the gifts as Christian *roles*.

The Roles

The Prophet Role

In the role of Prophet, God commands all Christians to speak the truth. "But speaking the truth in love, we are to grow up in all aspects into Him, who is the head even Christ. . . . Therefore laying aside all falsehood, speak truth each one of you, with his neighbor" (Ephesians 4:15, 25, NASB).

The Server Role

In the role of Server, God commands all Christians to serve one another. "For you were called to freedom, brethren; only do not turn your freedom into an opportunity for the flesh, but through love serve one another" (Galatians 5:13, NASB).

The Teacher Role

In the role of Teacher, all Christians are commanded to teach. "Let the word of Christ richly dwell within you, with all wisdom teaching and admonishing one another with psalms and hymns and spiritual songs" (Colossians 3:16, NASB). "Therefore go and make disciples of all nations . . . teaching them to obey everything I have commanded you" (Matthew 28:19).

The Exhorter Role

In the role of Exhorter, God commands all Christians to exhort one another. "But encourage [exhort] one another daily" (Hebrews 3:13). "Let us not give up meeting together, as some are in the habit of doing, but let us encourage one another" (Hebrews 10:25).

The Giver Role

In the role of Giver, all are commanded to give. "Give, and it will be given to you. A good measure, pressed down, shaken together and running over, will be poured into your lap" (Luke 6:38). "Freely you have received, freely give" (Matthew 10:8).

The Administrator Role

The role of Administrator is seen in principle in these verses: "Diligent hands will rule" (Proverbs 12:24). "He that is slow to anger is better than the mighty; and he that ruleth his spirit is better than he that taketh a city" (Proverbs 16:32, KJV). "But everything should be done in a fitting and orderly way" (1 Corinthians 14:40).

The Mercy Role

All Christians are commanded to function in the role of Mercy. "Blessed are the merciful, for they will be shown mercy" (Matthew 5:7). And concerning the mercy demonstrated by the Good Samaritan Jesus said: "Go and do likewise" (Luke 10:37).

Therefore, though one may have only one primary gift, this does not preclude one from functioning in the other gifts as roles. God has called all Christians to be like Christ. In fact, Christians are to be the visible manifestation of Christ to a lost and dying world. Therefore, as Christ expressed all of these gifts in His life and ministry, so too must Christians function in all of the roles as part of their calling.

Chapter 5

Gift Projection

Because a Motivational Gift is the very essence of one's personality, it is often difficult for a person to understand how others can see an issue differently than he or she sees it. In fact, to some, it is absolutely dumbfounding that others can understand a situation just as clearly as they themselves and yet come to different conclusions about the issue. With this in mind, it is easy to see that Christians far too often engage in what has been termed gift projection, i.e., imposing their particular gifts upon others.

Gift projection can often be seen in the actions of Prophet-motivated people. Because of their strong personalities, it seems that Prophets have a propensity toward gift projection. Prophets may demand that others be just as decisive about a given situation as they are. To Prophets things are either right or wrong, black or white, with no neutral or middle ground. Issues seem very clear to them. Because this is so, they often demand others to see things the way they see them and as quickly as they see them. They make quick moral decisions based upon outward, available information.[1] Prophets and Teachers may clash precisely at this point because Teachers may want to reserve their judgment until all the facts or data are known. In fact, Teachers may attempt to impose their cautious, reserved judgment upon the Prophet. So, gift projection is not limited to only those with the Motivational Gift of Prophet. In fact, every gift type has committed gift projection.

It is human nature to think that one's perspective is

the correct perspective. Thus, Christians often attempt to make others see things from their particular perspectives or through their particular "colored glasses."

Those with the Motivational Gift of Mercy, for instance, may attempt to project their gift upon others by demanding that people be more loving and compassionate. Exhorters may demand that others not be depressed regardless of the circumstances. In fact, the Exhorter may actually reprimand others for not "having the victory" over their present circumstances.

C. Peter Wagner calls gift projection a syndrome.[2] *The American Heritage Dictionary* describes a syndrome as,

> A group of symptoms that collectively indicate or characterize a disease, a psychological disorder, or another abnormal condition. A complex of symptoms indicating the existence of an undesirable condition or quality. [3]

Undoubtedly, gift projection is a complex of symptoms indicating the existence of an undesirable condition or quality. In that sense, then, *gift projection* is a syndrome. However, it is a syndrome which Christians can and must overcome.

God is the Author of the Differences

To the degree that one is willing to look at a specific situation from someone else's perspective, to that degree can gift projection be overcome. No one has the right to engage in gift projection. God has made the various members of His Church with differing functions and abilities. Thus, each member of the body of Christ will necessarily have *No one has the right to engage in gift projection.* his or her own perspective. Since God is the author of the differences, and of the various Motivational Gifts and personality types, we sin when we attempt to force others away from *their* God-given perspective and into *our* God-given perspective. Remember, God is the designer, and we are the design.

Saul and David: Example of Gift Projection

In an interesting interpretive application of David's refusal to wear Saul's armor—and in stark defiance of gift projection—Wagner says, "David refused to wear Saul's armor, and so do I."[4] What worked and was good for Saul during times of battle was not necessarily good for David. Had Saul succeeded in getting David to wear his armor during David's battle with Goliath, the results may have been disastrous for the young shepherd.

> Then Saul dressed David in his own tunic. He put a coat of armor on him and a bronze helmet on his head. David fastened on his sword over the tunic and tried walking around, because he was not used to them. "I cannot go in these," he said to Saul, "because I am not used to them." So he took them off (1 Sam. 17:38-39).

We must do as David did . . . "take them off." Cast off

the gift projections of other people. Do not allow others to tell you how you should behave with regard to your own personality structure.

The Falsification of Giftedness

As a psychologist, Carl Jung discussed the issue of "gift projection" from the perspective of outcome. He called the assumption or adoption of someone else's personality type, the "falsification of type."[5] Similarly, the assumption and adoption of another's Motivational Gift would be the "falsification of giftedness." Jung said that a person who labored under the "falsification of type" would later become neurotic as a result.

A neurotic person is prone to symptoms such as excessive anxiety or insecurity, depression, and irrational fears. The person may not have all of these symptoms, but he or she may display one or more of them on a consistent basis.

In my counseling, I have discovered that one way "falsification of giftedness" happens is through admiration. For example, many novice preachers have their "heroes in the faith." This is not bad in and of itself. However, sometimes when young preachers attempt to emulate their heroes, more than a simple mimicking occurs. Sometimes a "falsification of giftedness" takes place, and the young preachers find themselves struggling to function in an area for which they are not gifted. Thus, anxiety, insecurity, depression, and irrational fears can be the result.

Some people who have participated in the WGI have

confessed that they had attempted to function in someone else's giftedness. Some of them testified to becoming "free" (to be who they truly are) as a result of having discovered their giftedness through the Motivational Gifts Indicator. When they discovered their true giftedness and began to function therein, they immediately experienced a joy that helped them overcome their former neurosis. This practical real-life experience is also confirmed by Carl Jung's statement that once a person has the "falsification of type," he can be cured only by developing his true and natural personality type.[6]

We must be careful not to force others to respond or minister the way that *we* do. And, we should not allow ourselves to be forced into someone else's mold. Christians must honor and celebrate the differences that God has placed in the church. Christians must learn to rely on one another for various perspectives, which when unified make up the whole picture and complete the body of Christ.

There is another side to gift projection. Not only do Christians often try to impose their gift on others, but they also, at times, try to dissuade others from exercising their own particular gift. For instance, if people with the Teacher Motivation step out of their natural ability of logic and analysis into the realm of emotions (Mercy) and attempt to make important decisions based on feelings rather than logic, they may find that their choices are wrong. Choices based on emotions and feelings are not inherently wrong, but this method of making decisions *may be wrong* for the Teacher who has the God-given, innate ability to make decisions based on logic and facts.

Then, due to the failure to make good choices based on

emotions, the Teacher may try to convince a Mercy person that he or she too must not make decisions based on emotions or feelings because, according to the Teacher's experience, decisions thus based are doomed to fail. Ultimately, in this situation, Teachers will project their gift, but before they do, they will project their failure to function in the gift of Mercy. However, the Teacher must realize and accept the fact that the Mercy person is gifted by God to make decisions based precisely on emotions and feelings. One method of decision making is not wrong and the other right; they are just different.

Mercy people have learned to take into account the way they feel about a problem and how their decisions may affect others emotionally. God uses Mercy and deals with the person through his or her emotions and feelings. Thus, decisions based on feelings and emotions *for the Mercy person* generally turn out correct and successful.

However, the Teacher may make decisions based solely on the facts and data with no regard to personal likes or dislikes. Thus, Teachers may make a decision that they do not like emotionally, but they do so because it is the *logical thing to do.* Whereas those with the Mercy motivation may make a decision based strictly on their emotions. But, more often than not, the correct procedure of decision making for Mercy is, in fact, based on emotions and feelings. After all, this is how God made *Mercy* to function.

Just as strong-willed parents might impose their personality types onto their children ("falsification of type"), and the children can be cured only by learning and developing their unique personality types, so too Christian parents may unwittingly force their Motivational Gifts upon their children ("falsification of giftedness").

Not only are parents susceptible to the inclination of gift projection, but so too are those who are in respected positions of leadership. Because of their highly influential positions of leadership, pastors must be especially careful not to fall into the gift-projection syndrome. In interviewing various people for this research, I came across several people who felt "put-upon" by some of their pastors over the years to be and act more like the pastor. Some of them admitted that once the pastor resigned, or once they left the church and went to another church, they felt "free to be themselves."

Gift Larceny

In one interesting counseling case I had years ago, a young man so admired his pastor that when he took the *Walston Gifts Indicator*, he answered in ways that would be more in line with his pastor's personality than his own. After the young man listened to some of my lectures on the topic, and he and I specifically talked about gift projection, he requested to retake the WGI. This time his true motivational gift was discovered, and he realized that he had done just the opposite of gift "projection"; he had done a sort of "gift larceny."

"Gift larceny" is the act of attempting to be like someone else. This common problem often rectifies itself in time. As the person grows and matures in his or her own personality, the desire to be like someone else lessens and the person begins to "find" himself or herself. However, when people do not mature in personality growth, it may take counseling and a "discovery" of their true Motivational Gift before they are free to be all that God has made them to be.

The Equal Value of the Gifts

Closely associated with the syndrome of gift projection is the false idea that some gifts are more valuable than others (and some are less valuable than others). All gifts are of equal value in the overall economy of God. Certain gifts may be best at certain times and in certain circumstances, but all of the various gifts are equally valuable and necessary overall.

Paul explains this truth by saying that "God has arranged the parts in the body, every one of them, just as he wanted them to be" (1 Corinthians 12:18). Since it is God who has placed the various gifts in the Body, "just as he wanted them to be," they are equally valuable. No one has the right to attempt to change another person's giftedness. Paul clearly explains that all of the various gifts are necessary:

The eye cannot say to the hand, "I don't need you!" And the head cannot say to the feet, "I don't need you!" On the contrary, those parts of the body that seem to be weaker [perhaps, Mercy and Service, just to name two] are indispensable, and the parts that we think are less honorable we treat with special honor. And the parts that are unpresentable are treated with special modesty, while our presentable parts need no special treatment. But God has combined the members of the body and has given greater honor to the parts that lacked it, so that there should be no division in the body, but that its parts should have equal concern for each other. If one part suffers, every part suffers with it; if one part is honored, every part rejoices with it (1 Corinthians 12:21-26).

It is part of the fallen, egotistical condition of humans to believe that their gifts and personalities are the best and that all others should conform to their perspectives. God has determined that the value of each gift is equal, though different in function. Paul's metaphor of the human body shows that each member, and thus each gift, is precious and significant.

God has determined that the value of each gift is equal, though different in function.

The young man mentioned above who wanted to have his pastor's personality later confessed that he felt that he had sinned against God by not graciously accepting God's particular personality gift meant just for him. He felt that he had discredited and devalued the very gift of God. He now understood that all of the gifts have equal value, but different functions.

[1] However, when a prophet is operating in the ministry of a prophet (Ephesians 4:11), he is a speaker for God. During this *revelatory act of ministry*, the prophet does not depend upon the *outward, available information*; the "information" he receives and the words he speaks are from the Lord. However, it should *continuously* be remembered that N.T. (non-foundational) prophets can and do err. This is why Paul set guidelines for judging prophetic utterances (1 Corinthians 14:29). Therefore, a true prophet will gladly submit his prophecies to the Body of Christ for judgment, and he will be open to correction and instruction by others in the Body.

[2] C. Peter Wagner, *Spiritual Gifts Can Help Your Church Grow* (Ventura, Ca.: Regal Books, 1979), p. 160.

[3] *The American Heritage Dictionary of the English Language*, executive ed. Anne H. Soukhanov, s.v. "syndrome," (Boston, Ma.: Houghton Mifflin Company, 1992), p. 1821.

[4] Wagner, p. 161.

[5] Carl G. Jung, *Psychological Types* (Princeton, N.J.: Princeton University Press, 1976), p. 332.

[6] Ibid.

Chapter 6

Some Characteristic Traits
of the
Seven Motivational Gifts

The following are definitions of the Motivational Gifts and the descriptions of the traits or characteristics found in people having the various gifts. A study of people reveals particular behavioral characteristics that are peculiar to the various Motivational Gifts. The reverse is also true: a study of the Motivational Gifts reveals characteristics that are peculiar to the various personality types among people. Thus, as you read the various descriptions of the characteristics of the Motivational Gifts, you may clearly see your own particular behavioral characteristics in the description of the characteristics of one, or more, of the Motivational Gifts.

One important thing to remember is that these gifts are not to be confused with the ministry gifts of Ephesians 4, nor the manifestations of the Spirit in 1 Corinthians 12. For instance, a person may have the Motivational Gift of Teacher but might not work in a job or ministry as a teacher. The outcome is that this person will do his job or ministry—whatever it is—through the eyes and analytical characteristics of a teacher. The "personality filter" of teacher is, in essence, the "rose-colored glasses" through which that person will see his or her world.

Another significant fact to keep in mind while reading the various descriptions below is that there are, most likely, no human expressions of the "pure" gifts. This means that, as mentioned above, the auxiliary, tertiary, and remaining motivational gifts have an effect in one way or another on the primary gifts. No person exercises a primary gift in a vacuum, i.e., solely by itself. Many things either help or hinder the expression of one's giftedness. However, the various gifts below are presented in their "pure" sense for purposes of clarification and classification. Therefore, one should realize that while these definitions and characteristics are appropriate for these gifts, a person's primary gift may not demonstrate all the characteristics intrinsic to that gift.

Rate Yourself

As you read through the descriptions of gift characteristics, rate yourself according to the traits. If you read, for instance, the characteristics of Prophet and you identify with all of the traits described therein, rate yourself a Five (5). If you do not see yourself in any of the characteristics of Prophet, rate yourself a One (1).

At the end of each gift's description, I shall place these words: **RATE Yourself (circle one) 1 - 2 - 3 - 4 - 5.** You should circle the number that you feel best fits you. Also, do not forget to consider the Pitfall Traits. Sometimes people see themselves in the negative traits of the gifts as well as in the positive ones.

Before you rate yourself, it would be beneficial if you read the characteristics of all seven gifts one time. Then, go back and read it again, rating yourself as you read it a second time. People often identify with a gift and circle a high number only to discover a little later that they actually identify even more with another gift. So, if you read them twice and rate yourself the second time through, you will have a better grasp of the gifts and how you identify (or don't identify) with them.

In chapter ten, you will take the WGI. It is there that you may be more accurate in learning your giftedness. However, even in this chapter, you can begin making progress toward that goal.

Prophet (Truth Teller) Characteristics

When people have the *Motivational Gift* of Prophet, it does not mean that they are prophets in the Old Testament or Ephesians 4:11 sense. It means rather, that they will have a "personality filter" or characteristics much as a prophet of God would have. The word "prophet" means simply one who speaks forth or openly, and in some cases this person speaks openly for God.

Truth Teller is another title that can be applied to the Motivational Gift of Prophet. The basic meaning of the word "prophecy" is "to speak forth," and biblically it signifies that one is "speaking forth" the mind or counsel of God. People often simply equate prophecy with prediction, but the primary meaning of prophecy is not prediction (fore-telling) but simply speaking openly (forth-telling). Furthermore, the use of the term Prophet in the Motivational Gifts sense does not mean nor connote prediction at all.

The Prophet's (or Truth-teller's) number one characteristic is boldly speaking the truth as he or she perceives it to be, with little or no fear of reprisal. People with the Prophet Motivation tend to be brutally frank when they explain their beliefs. For some people, the reason for their honest frankness is that they see themselves as those who speak for God and for His truth.

People with the Prophet Motivation tend to be brutally frank when they explain their beliefs.

However, this does not mean that prophets are infallible. Prophets can and do make mistakes. Those who are Prophet Motivated must be submitted to the church leadership, and they must be willing to be corrected by their brothers and sisters in the Body. True prophets want their words to be tested, and mature prophets admit when they are wrong.

Another chief characteristic of people with the Motivation of Prophet is that they see things as either "black or white" and right or wrong. For the Prophet, sin is sin and righteousness is righteousness; there are no "gray" or neutral areas. Thus, they are very blunt and honest about sin, or about what they *perceive* to be sin. This black-or-white attitude is often so overwhelming that some non-prophet-motivated people find it difficult and unsettling to be around them.

Prophets are open and honest about almost everything. If a Prophet is asked what he or she thinks about something from ecology to ethics or fashion to fascism, it is fairly certain the Prophet will give an honest, open, and blunt answer.

Prophets desire to convey God's Word verbally. They generally have good communicative ability and can use it to express God's Word. They *enjoy* speaking out what God has given them to speak.

Another thing that can make it uncomfortable for some to be around Truth Tellers (i.e., Prophets) is they sometimes have the ability to "see-through" and discern the motives of others.[1] This can be disastrous for the hypocrite. However, a caution should be raised at this point. Young, immature people with the Motivational Gift of Prophet may only *think* that they can discern the motives of others but in fact be wrong. Thus, just because people have the Motivational Gift of Prophet does not automatically mean that they will always be able to "see-through" the motives of others. This discerning quality of the Prophet is developed with maturity, both emotional and spiritual, and by a continual dependence upon the Holy Spirit. Furthermore, this discerning ability does not enable the Prophet to discern every person's motive in every situation.

Those with the Prophet Motivation believe that the lifestyle of Christians should outwardly (demonstratively) display the fruits of righteousness. In other words, they desire that people show forth their Christianity in godly and holy conduct. Anything less than an outward godly and holy conduct, according to the Prophet's standards, is considered by the Prophet as grounds to question a person's spirituality. Also, the Prophet detests any and all forms of hypocrisy, or perceived hypocrisy.

They tend to be very open to God concerning their own sin, and they are quick to repent. They want all sin out of their life so that they may serve Jesus with all of their heart, soul, and mind. Often, they will verbalize their own experience of sin and repentance so that others may learn from their mistakes and be broken before God for their sins too.[2] Wagner says that Prophets tend to be politically-minded.[3] Reminiscent of the Old Testament prophets, they are highly opinionated with regard to public righteousness, politics, and contemporary culture.[4] This being so, Prophets often stay informed of social trends both nationally and internationally.

Prophet Pitfalls

There are some pitfalls for people with the Prophet Motivation, as there are with all the gifts. Sometimes in the their effort to get people to repent, they may actually alienate people by preaching "too strong" a message or by being too blunt in even general conversation with others. Often, Truth-tellers tend to lack tactfulness in their rebuke.

I remember once having dinner with a very strongly Prophet-Motivated person. There were six people at the table, and the "prophet" knew only me. All of the other folks were perfect strangers to him, except for my introductions. Before the dinner was over, the Prophet had managed to offend nearly every last person at the table. Yet, he did not have a clue that his questioning of the dinner companions and then telling them what was "wrong" with their lives was out of line in the least. He felt entirely justified to have spoken the "truth" (as he perceived it to be) with great gusto.

Also, people with the Motivation of Prophet will sometimes be very "standoffish" and hard to get to know. The reason for this is that they see, through their particular "colored glasses," people as groups rather than as individuals with individual needs. They will preach a strong message to the group, let the chips fall where they may, and not stick around to help see that the principles of their teaching are put into practice in individual lives.

Finally, from the extremely negative side, these people have been known to be dogmatic, arrogant, harsh, intimidating, overbearing, and unbending. The mature Prophet, while having a strong personality, will have mastered these negative traits. Not every person with the Motivation of Prophet necessarily has all of these negative characteristics, but they may fall prey to them if they are not careful. **Rate Yourself (circle one) 1 - 2 - 3 - 4 - 5**

Server Characteristics

A Server Motivated person is one whose nature is to serve others in a tangible and practical way. People who have the Motivational Gift of Service are motivated to meet the practical needs of others. They often feel that love is demonstrated by the outward act of helping people in

People who have the Motivational Gift of Service are motivated to meet the practical needs of others.

need. Servers also have a desire to perform manual tasks for the glory of God. Thus, they are helpful around the church with menial tasks. In fact, the word *service* mainly connotes menial, ordinary tasks. The Greek word from which the word service (deacon) comes is *diakonia* and means minister or servant. People with the Motivation of Service are able to detect the needs of others in the realm of the physical. If there is a need, i.e., something needs to be done or fixed, the Servers will be alert to it and quick to act. Service is a task-oriented gift. Though Servers may in fact help individual people, they are *motivated by the task* that is involved in helping the person. A great desire of the Server is to help meet needs as quickly as possible. They often have the ability to work long hours helping others. Truly, the Server takes to heart the idea that he is his brother's keeper. In every church or group of people there are always physical needs. Servers have the ability to meet those needs.

Servers are quite often misjudged as non-spiritual because their attention is directed toward the more physical, here-and-now, tasks of life. One Server I know is a gifted handyman. When there are physical tasks to be done at his church (like building a set or stage for a play), he is often the first person to volunteer to help. Yet, he seems to be the last person in the prayer meeting. However, Server-Motivated people may not show their spirituality in the same way as others do. The Servers' spirituality may not be as visible as the pastor's, but they *are* engaged in spiritual activities by functioning in the gift that God has given to them. It is far too easy and wrong to decide that one person is "spiritual" because he or she prays loudly and appears pious while the Server is not spiritual because he or she is engaged not in prayer but in using hammers, cooking, sewing, mechanics, and various other tools of service.

Server Pitfalls

There are also pitfalls of which the Server must be aware. Servers can become so involved in the physical realm that they tend to forget the need for the spiritual.

Sometimes, because they are alert to the needs of others, they may attempt to help people even before they realize that they have a problem. So, caution is in order for the Server. Also, the Server may become very critical of other people who are not "serving" as he or she thinks they should.

If a certain person does not seem to be a server, helping others in a tangible and practical way, the Server may question the genuineness of that person's love (sometimes their love of both others and God). Servers do not necessarily have all of these negative qualities. However they should be aware of these pitfalls and be careful not to fall into them. **Rate Yourself (circle one) 1 - 2 - 3 - 4 - 5**

Teacher Characteristics

The Teacher is one who thinks in a logical and analytical fashion and thus communicates from that rationale. The term teacher is from the Greek word *didasko* and means literally "to teach" or "to give instruction." People who have the Teacher Motivation will be in the habit of investigating and validating truth for themselves. Teachers do not simply believe something because the *evangelist* or *preacher* said it; they want to double-check and verify it. They will often test the knowledge of those who teach them. They may desire to know what formal education or teaching

To the Teacher, truth is even higher and more desirable than unity and peace.

credentials the instructor has. Also, the Teacher places an importance on words and on their proper usage. Concerning study, the Teacher is very meticulous; each detail is savored for its importance, and teachers also place a great importance on facts and truth. While peace and unity are desirable conditions for life and living, to the Teacher, *truth* is even higher and more desirable than unity and peace.

People with the Teacher Motivation receive as much joy in researching and knowing truth as they do in presenting it. Finally, they feel that their burden is to convey truth, while the burden of receiving the truth belongs to that of the hearers.

Although not all who have the Motivational Gift of Teacher are in positions of formal teaching, it would be good if those who have this primary Motivation were urged to enter some type of formal training, and then exercise their teaching gift after their training. Because their primary motivation is intellectual and facts oriented, they become capable teachers when given the proper opportunities and training.

Teacher Pitfalls

There are pitfalls that the Teacher must guard against. Because of a love for details, the Teacher may sometimes leave the main topic during a presentation to discuss theoretical points, which seem to have little or no relevance to the subject at hand. Also, because they sometimes give such attention to details and precise definitions, their presentations may appear to lack a certain warmth and personableness.

A primary pitfall of many with the Teacher Motivation is pride. They may become overly proud of their knowledge and their ability to discover truth. This negative characteristic has been borne out on several occasions in my presence. Knowing that this sort of pride is wrong, some Teacher-Motivated people have smiled in happy agreement with the fact that they are prideful about their ability to discover and know truth! Some feel that they are part of an *elite* (almost esoteric) "club." Some teachers have complained that less-perceptive people cannot "track" with them. This problem of "tracking" is compounded if the Teacher is an introvert who is shy to speak out and be verbally clear.

Another problem may arise when Teacher-Motivated people are students. They may *test* the knowledge of those who teach him. Sometimes a Teacher-Motivated person will actually inquire of the teacher's educational credentials. When this is being done, Teacher-Motivated people may appear to be proud and arrogant when in reality they are not; they just simply want to know. **Rate Yourself (circle one) 1 - 2 - 3 - 4 - 5**

Exhorter Characteristics

The Exhorter is one who encourages others to reach new spiritual heights. They often urge others to pursue some course of action that is prospective, looking to the future. The Exhorter's perspective differs from the person with the Mercy Motivation in that the Exhorter looks forward and encourages others to look to the future whereas Mercy persons attempt to comfort, which is retrospective, having to do with something already experienced. The Exhorter has the God-given ability to comfort and encourage others.

The Exhorter has the God-given ability to comfort and encourage others.

Exhorters are people-centered, and they enjoy counseling others one-on-one. Kenneth Gangel points out that while there is no "gift of counseling," those who are gifted in exhortation (*paraklesis*) may very well become counselors.[5] However, it should not be inferred that only people who are in some position of counseling are Exhorters. This gift is distributed throughout the Body of Christ, and many laypeople (as well as many in leadership) have this gift.

The Exhorter's "colored glasses" cause them to see people as individuals rather than as parts of a larger group. Thus, they feel more comfortable speaking to people on a one-on-one basis rather than in a group setting. They make good counselors because they enjoy helping people understand and take appropriate steps of action to achieve a given goal. They have the ability to see answers in the Bible for human problems. Exhorters have the desire to help people rise to new levels of spirituality. They are quick to speak words of encouragement, usually words that confirm a good prospect ahead; e.g., "Hang in there; it will all work out"; "God isn't finished with you yet," or "You are going to be a better person because of all this tribulation."

Exhorters may even *enjoy* times of personal tribulation because they feel it will produce in them higher levels of spirituality. This is also expressed to others who are going through difficult times. Exhorters have the ability to see serious problems and setbacks as avenues to spiritual growth. The Exhorters' "motto" could very well be: *"That which does not kill us makes us stronger."*

Exhorter Pitfalls

Exhorters may fall prey to the pitfall of over dependence on the people they minister to. Sometimes Exhorters need to feel that their counseling is being well received. If they do not receive this feedback, it can be emotionally distressing for them.

Because Exhorters can arrive at positive solutions to many problems and because they like to encourage others to rise to new levels of spiritual maturity, Exhorters may tend to be very dominant and appear to others as self-acclaimed know-it-alls. Exhorters may often appear to be unsympathetic to people in their present distress because they encourage people to look ahead, and thus downplay their present difficulties. It is precisely here that Mercy and Exhorters may clash. Mercy motivated people almost never downplay a person's present struggles whereas the Exhorter might say, "Oh, it's no big deal. You are going to grow because of this." The Mercy person, however, may actually cry with the distressed individual and in so doing confirm that it is a "big deal." Also, Exhorters can get so caught up in helping a person they may forget that there are other people who need them as well, particularly their own family.

Again, the pitfalls are just that: pitfalls. Exhorters do

not necessarily have all of these negative traits, but Exhorters must guard themselves against them. **Rate Yourself (circle one) 1 - 2 - 3 - 4 - 5**

Giver Characteristics

Givers are motivated to give to God. They do this by generously sharing their personal material and financial assets with ministries and people in need.

This Motivational Gift is described by the Greek word *metadidomi* which means "to give a share of" or "to impart." This particular form of "sharing" is distinct from and different than simply giving something away. The *metadidomi* form of giving actually means to share. The apostle Paul used this word when he said, "I long to see you so that I may impart [*metadidomi*] to you some spiritual gift to make you strong—that is, that you and I may be *mutually* encouraged by each other's faith" (emphasis added, Romans 1:11-12). Paul does not intend to simply give away a gift that he has, but rather he desires to *share* some gift with the Romans. The point is that the Motivational Gift of Giving is more than simply *giving away* something. Givers *share* what they have with others in need.

In the act of sharing what they have, Givers also share a part of themselves. Givers give generously of their finances and material goods, and in so doing they actually become partakers with the person or ministry to

In the act of sharing what they have, Givers also share a part of themselves.

whom they give. This truth separates the role of giving, which all Christians are called to, from the Motivational Gift of Giving which only some are called and equipped to perform. Thus, when those who do not have the Motivational Gift of Giving give to others or to a ministry, they may in fact give *away* what they have.

Example: A Christian, acting in the Christian *role* of giving, may give to a person or to a ministry and never once again think of that person or ministry. This is often true in missionary services where there is an appeal for finances for a particular missionary or missions outreach. Christians who do not have the gift of giving may be moved to give during the missionary service because a financial need has been brought to their attention. However, when they give, it may be a very "mechanical" process. For example, I have given to people and ministries during various appeals for finances. However, more often than not, after my duty was discharged and the finances were given, I simply forgot which particular person or enterprise it was that I had given to. However, Motivational Givers do not *give-and-forget*. Givers not only give their finances or other material assets, but they give a part of themselves through their act of sharing. Givers *share* (rather than simply *give it away*) what they have and who they are with those in need.

Paul says in 1 Thessalonians 2:8: "We loved you so much that we were delighted to share with you not only the gospel of God but our lives as well, because you had become so dear to us." Again, he did not *give away* the gospel and his life so that he no longer had these, but he "gave" them in a way that he, Paul, became a part of the believers in Thessalonica. This kind of sharing may be likened to the act of sharing the fire from a burning torch. A person with a burning torch may share his or her fire by lighting another person's unlit torch. The second torch has now received fire, and the first torch is still burning.

Givers cannot fathom hoarding their personal assets because they realize that all they own has come to them from the gracious hand of God. Thus, they are aware that God—not their jobs or ministries—is their source. Givers recognize that it all belongs to God, and the Giver is a human conduit through which God blesses other people.

In spite of what might be considered a logical assumption, the gift of Giving is not appointed only to the wealthy. People from all economic strata are given the gift of Giving.

Givers are keenly aware of the financial needs of other people and ministries and delight in meeting those needs. They are willing to own less than they have access to if it means it will advance the Kingdom of God and help others in need. When mature Givers give to ministries or to people in need, they generally do it quietly with no need of recognition. Also, Givers generally have the ability to manage their own finances in such a way that they always seem to have enough for themselves and for others who may be in need.

Giver Pitfalls

Givers must be aware of certain pitfalls. They are sometimes taken advantage of by people who are less than honest. But even after such unfortunate circumstances, the Giver is usually undaunted and will continue to give, often indiscriminately. Charles Bryant tells of an incident in which a Giver was conned into giving $20,000 to benefit a sick child in need of major surgery. Later, it was discovered that the sick child did not exist and the Giver lost all $20,000. When the truth was explained to the Giver, he was overjoyed that there was no suffering child and was not concerned at all that he had lost such a large sum of money.[6] Thus, the Giver may be a "soft touch" and end up giving to anybody with a sad (or hard-luck) story.

Another pitfall is that the Giver may judge other Christians' spirituality by their material assets and finances. They may reason that since God uses them in the area of giving, He must also supply them with the assets to give. Therefore, if others do not have material wealth, it is because God cannot trust them. Thus a lack of assets is seen as the direct result of a lack of spirituality.

Givers may also inadvertently perpetuate spiritual immaturity in others. They do this by becoming the source for other Christians in need instead of letting the person seek God for the answers. It behooves Givers to remember that *always* meeting the needs of others is *not* always the will of God. **Rate Yourself (circle one) 1 - 2 - 3 - 4 - 5**

Administrator Characteristics

An Administrator (Leader, NAS; Leadership, NIV; Ruler, KJV) is one who thinks from a managerial perspective and desires to coordinate and direct people and activities. The word *Administrator* is from the Greek word *proistemi* and literally means "to stand before," or "to lead." The Administrator is a leader who *enjoys* coordinating activities or projects for the purpose of reaching a common goal. Administrators have the ability to organize things or people within a job or ministry to produce the highest efficiency. They are good at defining long-range goals and can relate those goals to others. Also, Administrators have a knowledge of the resources needed to reach goals, and they will desire to reach those goals as quickly and efficiently as possible.

Administrators have the ability to organize things or people within a job or ministry.

Another trait of Administrators is that they *enjoy* being responsible for a job, task, or project; they like to know that they are in control of a situation. The Administrator also has the ability to delegate authority. Neatness and organization are keynotes of these people's lifestyle at home, on the job, in the ministry, and even in their dress. If they have a desk, everything will be neatly in order; every paper clip, every rubber band, every pencil, etc., will all be in their proper places.

Administrator Pitfalls

One of the major pitfalls of Administrators is that they may overly enjoy the feeling of controlling a situation and thus allow their authority to become oppressive to those under them. They may also fall into the trap of overly controlling people and projects.

Another pitfall of which Administrators must be aware is that they may not want to delegate authority because they feel that they are the only one capable of doing the job correctly. When this happens, they tend to overload themselves with work beyond their physical capabilities.

Sometimes Administrators feel that the task to be completed is so important that they will use people as "tools," with little or no regard for their emotions, to get the job accomplished. Surprisingly, this may be especially true for those Administrators whose job is ministry related. Any time a project is "for the Lord," it carries with it an inherent quality of importance. Thus, the temptation to use others to accomplish the task at hand is heightened and must be resisted. It should be remembered by all administrators (and any leader in the Christian church) that the Bible teaches servant leadership. **Rate Yourself (circle one) 1 - 2 - 3 - 4 - 5**

Mercy Characteristics

The person with the Mercy Motivation is one whose nature is to sympathize with the misery of others. The Mercy motivated person is one who desires to comfort and help people who are in emotional distress. The word mercy comes from the Greek word *eleeo*, and it means to feel sympathy for or to feel the misery of others. Also, Mercy is not only a feeling, but it is manifested outwardly in acts of mercy or sympathy.

The Mercy motivated person is one who desires to comfort and help people who are in emotional distress.

A major characteristic of Mercy-people is that they

will avoid, at almost all costs, hurting someone's feelings. The emotional status of others is of paramount importance to those with the Mercy Motivation.

They often identify with the emotional status of others so deeply that they can actually experience the pain of the other person. If their friends are happy, they will be happy with them. If their friends are sad, the person with Mercy will truly *share* in their sadness.

While others may, and should by God's grace, try to comfort people in distress, Mercy motivated people have the gifted *ability* to comfort others. Thus, even though we all may, and should, demonstrate mercy to others to the best of our abilities—"Blessed are the merciful, for they will be shown mercy"—the Mercy Motivation is a gift from God that is given only to certain members of the Body of Christ. Mercy differs from the Server in that the person of Mercy desires to help those with emotional problems while Servers desire to help those with physical problems. People with the Mercy Motivation have a keen awareness of the emotional atmosphere of a group. They can walk into a room of people and immediately perceive the emotion of the group. Finally, the Mercy person desires to relieve the hurting person's misery as soon as possible.

Mercy Pitfalls

Perhaps the greatest pitfall for those with the Mercy Motivation is that they may become too emotionally minded at the expense of logic.

Also, they may fall into the trap of identifying with others so much of the time that they begin to lose contact with how they feel as individuals.

Next, the Mercy person may be overly critical of and not get along with the "Prophet." The reason for this is that Mercy may see the Prophet as unfeeling, unloving, and far too harsh.

Finally, they may tend to be far too lenient with Christians in sin, because they may attempt to sympathize with them in their time of distress rather than dealing with the question of sin. Consequently, timely discipline may be ignored. **Rate Yourself (circle one) 1 - 2 - 3 - 4 - 5**

Summary

As stated above, the descriptions of the Motivations herein are stark in that they are descriptions of the *singular* gifts. And, it is doubtful that anyone has a one-dimensional personality. However, every person will have one of these Motivational Gifts predominantly as his or her personality type. Thus, you may see your "reflection" in more than one of these gifts, but generally your "reflection" will be more apparent in one particular motivation than any other.

Some people identify with nearly all of the characteristics of a particular Motivation and almost not at all with any of the remaining six. Others find it difficult to determine which is their primary Motivation because they identify with two or three of them.

Note: If you rated yourself on the gifts as you read through them, which one was the highest? The second? And the third? You can list them below:

Primary _____

Auxiliary _____

Tertiary _____

[1] Please understand, this is not the gift of *discernings of spirits* as in 1 Corinthians 12.

[2] Bill Gothard, *How To Understand Spiritual Gifts* (Oak Brook, Il.: Institute in Basic Life Principles, 1981), p. 63, cf. also Bryant, p. 110.

[3] Wagner, p. 230.

[4] Ibid.

[5] Kenneth O. Gangel, *Unwrap Your Spiritual Gifts* (Wheaton, Il.: Victor Books, 1988), p. 34.

[6] Bryant, p. 87.

Chapter 7

Biblical Personality Examples of the Seven Motivational Gifts

Throughout the Scripture there are various men and women of God who demonstrated the gifts. These people serve as examples to us. Here is a small sampling of some key characters through whom these gifts were manifested.

Prophet

The Apostle Paul

The Apostle Paul is an excellent example of the motivation of Prophet. In Galatians, Paul had to deal with a brother who had gotten himself sidetracked from the gospel of grace. This brother was the great Apostle Peter. Even though it was Peter, Paul spoke the truth to him not fearing the reprisals that could have come from such a confrontation. In Galatians 2:11, Paul says, *"But when Peter came to Antioch, I opposed him to his face, because he was in the wrong."* Notice the two main points of Paul's words. First, he opposed Peter. Prophets will always oppose sin wherever or in whomever it is found. Second, he says, "to his face." These people are known for their ability to confront people face to face. Generally, Prophets will say nothing in secret that they would not say openly to the individual concerned. Prophets will speak the truth (as they perceive it to be) without fear of others because they

> *Prophets will always oppose sin wherever or in whomever it is found.*

have a holy fear of the living God.

Another example of Paul's strong Prophet Motivation is seen in the "John Mark situation" (for more about the John Mark situation, see **Barnabas**, under **Exhorter** below). Paul, through the "rose-colored glasses" of a Prophet, made a value judgment of the ministry of John Mark. Paul seeing through the personality filter of the Prophet Motivation, wanted to exclude John Mark from a particular ministry because he had failed to complete a prior missionary trip. As far as Paul was concerned John Mark had failed and that was that; John Mark's ministry was over (Acts 15:36-41).

One of the pitfalls that a prophet may fall into is that he or she may expose sin without restoring the sinner. Paul seems to have fallen into this pitfall in the case of John Mark. Thus, Paul was very harsh toward what he perceived to be sin. Paul was so harsh, in fact, that it appears that he saw no restoration in sight for young John Mark.

John The Baptist

It is obvious that John the Baptist had the Motivational Gift of Prophet. Just as any prophet of the Old Testament that could be cited, John identified sin, exposed it openly, and called people to a life of righteousness. John saw the world in stark contrasts; things, actions, and motives were black and white, right and wrong. John, like most Truth-Tellers, saw little (if any) middle-ground.

People with the Motivation of Prophet will speak the truth in the face of personal hardship, and John was no exception. Even though John faced imprisonment and ultimately death, he still spoke the truth openly and bluntly. He exposed the sin of Herod who was having an adulterous affair with his brother's wife, and John paid for that exposé with his life.

Server

Martha

Martha is well known as Mary's sister who was busy attending to the physical needs of her guests while Mary simply sat at the feet of Jesus. One can imagine Martha cooking, setting the table, making sure everything was ready. But it did not set well with her that Mary was not helping. Luke says:

> As Jesus and his disciples were on their way, he came to a village where a woman named Martha opened her home to him. She had a sister called Mary, who sat at the Lord's feet listening to what he said. But Martha was distracted by all the preparations that had to be made. She came to him and asked, "Lord, don't you care that my sister has left me to do the work by myself? Tell her to help me!" "Martha, Martha," the Lord answered, "you are worried and upset about many things, but only one thing is needed. Mary has chosen what is better, and it will not be taken away from her" (Luke 10:38-42).

Martha had fallen into two pitfalls, and Jesus corrected her on both. Martha became so involved in the physical realm that she seemed to forget the need for the spiritual.

As one reads this story, one might assume that Jesus will tell Martha to stop doing what she was doing and join with Mary in sitting at his feet. But, that assumption would be wrong. Interestingly, Jesus gently corrects Martha concerning her "gift projection" onto Mary without demanding that Martha change her basic personality.

Furthermore, Jesus tells her that she is "worried and upset about many things." He did not say, "Don't be a server Martha." He did say, however, don't be "worried and upset" about these things. There is a balance to be had. Serve, but do so in joy. If you are worried and upset, you've gone too far. There should be a joy in the exercise of one's gift.

John's Gospel says simply that Martha served. "Here a dinner was given in Jesus' honor. Martha served, while Lazarus was among those reclining at the table with him" *Jesus did not disapprove of Martha's activities.* (John 12:2). So, in this wonderful account, we can see the server's heart in that she was attempting to serve the guest of honor, and at the same time, the account teaches that there is to be a balance in the exercise of one's gifts. Some have argued that Jesus told Martha to stop her business and sit at his feet. But, this was not the case. Jesus did not disapprove of Martha's activities, and He did not project someone else's gift onto her. He just wanted her to learn how to exercise her Serving gift in joy and peace without projecting her personality onto others.

Timothy

Timothy is another example of one with the Motivation of Server. Paul says of Timothy:

> I hope in the Lord to send Timothy to you soon, that I also may be cheered when I receive news about you. I have no one else like him, who takes a genuine interest in your welfare. For everyone looks out for his own interests, not those of Jesus Christ. But you know that Timothy has proved himself, because as a son with his father he has served me in the work of the gospel (Philippians 2:22).

First, Paul notes Timothy's unique ministry of service in that he says that he has no one else like him. Second, it appears that Timothy was serving Paul in such a way that it allowed Paul the opportunity and freedom to carry out his own ministry. Paul says that Timothy proved himself in his ministry by serving him as a son serves a father.

Timothy had the Motivational Gift of Service, and he exercised that giftedness according to the will of God for the purpose of spreading the gospel. (Also, the gift of Teacher seems to have been part of Timothy's PAT-Mix— 1 Timothy 4:6-16; 2 Timothy 2:1-2, 4:2-4.)

Teacher

Apollos

A man named Apollos appears in the book of Acts. Apollos is a good example of the motivation of Teacher.

Now a certain Jew named Apollos . . . came to Ephesus; and he was mighty in the Scriptures. This man had been instructed in the way of the Lord; and being fervent in spirit, he was speaking and teaching accurately the things concerning Jesus, being acquainted only with the baptism of John; and he began to speak out boldly in the synagogue. But when Priscilla and Aquila heard him, they took him aside and explained to him the way of God more accurately . . . . when he [Apollos] had arrived, he helped greatly those who had believed through grace; for he powerfully refuted the Jews in public, demonstrating by the Scriptures that Jesus was the Christ (Acts 18:24-28, NASB).

Notice some of the traits of the Teacher in this man Apollos. First, he was mighty in the Scriptures. Thus, he was a *studier* of the Word of God. Second, he was speaking and teaching *accurately* the way of the Lord. He was careful about details. Third, he was open and teachable, for others explained the way of God more accurately to him. Last, he helped greatly those who had believed by teaching from the Scriptures that Jesus was the Christ. He taught others.

Luke

It appears that Luke also had the Motivational Gift of Teacher. As pointed out in the last chapter, teachers typically need to (1) investigate and validate truth for themselves. They do not believe something simply because someone else told them. Also, Teachers are (2) logical and analytical. Thus, when they present information either in teaching or writing, they tend to share their information systematically and in an orderly sequence. Furthermore, Teachers are motivated to (3) confirm and validate truth not only for themselves, but for those whom they may instruct. All three of these points are present in the opening verses of Luke's Gospel.

Teachers typically need to investigate and validate truth for themselves.

> Many have undertaken to draw up an account of the things that have been fulfilled among us, just as they were handed down to us by those who from the first were eyewitnesses and servants of the word. Therefore, since *I myself have carefully investigated everything from the beginning*, it seemed good also to me to write *an orderly account* for you, most excellent Theophilus, so that *you may know the certainty of the things you have been taught* (emphasis added, Luke 1:1-4).

Exhorter

Priscilla and Aquila

Priscilla and Aquila seem to have the motivation of Exhorter. For they encouraged Apollos and led him to a higher level of spiritual understanding. "But when Priscilla and Aquila heard him, they took him aside and explained to him the way of God more accurately" (Acts 18:26, NASB).

Barnabas

Perhaps the prime example of an Exhorter is Barnabas. Barnabas was originally called Joseph, but it appears that the apostles identified his gift of Exhortation and nicknamed him accordingly. "Joseph, a Levite from Cyprus, *whom the apostles called Barnabas* (which means Son of Encouragement), sold a field he owned and brought the money and put it at the apostles' feet" (emphasis added, Acts 4:36).

Speaking of Joseph's name change, Stanley Horton says that the phrase "son of" was used to indicate a person's *character* or *nature*.[1] The apostles renamed Joseph and now called him the "Son of Encouragement." The word Encouragement is the Greek word *paraklesis* and is the same word that is translated *Exhortation* in Romans 12:8. What Joseph *did* was a natural outgrowth of who he was. His character or personality type was that of an Exhorter. His Motivational Gift was Exhortation. He fulfilled the will of God by exercising his God-given gift. He did this by simply doing what was natural for him. He encouraged others so effectively that the apostles nicknamed him accordingly.

The Son of Exhortation also displayed his Motivational Gift in his ministry to the church in Antioch. A new fellowship of Gentile believers had developed in Antioch and when the church in Jerusalem heard of it, they sent Barnabas to them. The establishment of this new fellowship of believers in Antioch was a very important event in the spreading of the gospel. Even the city of Antioch itself was significant because it was the third most important city in the entire Roman empire. Only Rome and Alexandria exceeded Antioch's importance.[2] Thus, since this was a very important event (i.e., the Gentiles becoming believers), and this was a very important place (Antioch), the Jerusalem church recognized the great importance of the event and sent their top exhorter, Barnabas, to encourage the new believers in Antioch (Acts 11:22-26).

The gift of Exhortation through Barnabas is also seen as reaching out to, or ministering to, one individual. Whereas Barnabas was sent to many, i.e., the church of Antioch, to minister encouragement, he also ministered the gift of Exhortation to one single individual, John Mark.

Paul and Barnabas had ministered together for some time, and in Acts 15 Paul suggested that he and Barnabas go back to visit the converts in the churches which were established during their first missionary journey in Cyprus and South Galatia. Barnabas was willing to do so but wanted to take John Mark (his cousin) along with them.

Paul, however, seeing through the "colored-glasses" of the Prophet Motivation did not want John Mark to accompany them because John Mark had failed to complete a tour of missionary duty earlier of which Paul and Barnabas were a part. Paul obviously felt that John Mark was unworthy because of his earlier failure, and Paul thought that John Mark was not dependable.

Barnabas, however, seeing through the "colored-glasses" of the Exhortation Motivation had decided to encourage John Mark by giving him another chance. This was such a hot issue between Paul and Barnabas that they *argued and separated* over it!

The outcome was that Paul took Silas and went to South Galatia. Barnabas, however, took John Mark and went back to Cyprus. Stanley Horton points out that the decision of Barnabas to take John Mark to Cyprus was wise because John Mark had been faithful in that territory.[3] Barnabas did not just attempt to encourage John Mark, but he was wise in his ministry of exhortation allowing John Mark the greater chance of success by taking him back to Cyprus.

Furthermore, it is important to note that Barnabas *the Exhorter* saw something that Paul the Prophet did not see: John Mark's potential. Paul, viewing the situation through the "colored glasses" of the Prophet Motivation, made a judgment on John Mark, found him lacking the necessary qualifications, and simply dismissed him from ministry. Barnabas, however, because of his Motivation of Exhortation, though having the same knowledge of John Mark's failure, saw John Mark's potential. Barnabas encouraged John Mark, and helped him pursue a course of conduct that reaffirmed his calling and looked forward to future ministry.

Barnabas' ministry of exhortation unto John Mark was eventually validated and even the Apostle Paul later thought better of John Mark. Barnabas' God-given character as an Exhorter was proved to be accurately ministered in the life and ministry of John Mark. Paul himself confirms this very fact when he later asked that Timothy bring John Mark with him because John Mark was "useful for ministry" (2 Timothy 4:11). So, in the mind of Paul, John Mark went from being *useless* to being *useful* and all of this may have been due to the encouragement that came to him from Barnabas, the Son of Encouragement.

Giver

The Philippian Church

The Philippian Church, or, perhaps more precisely, some of the members in the church, seem to have had the Giver Motivation. Perhaps the elder in charge of the Philippian Church was a Giver, and thus the church was a giving church. Often a church will take on the main characteristic of the ruling elder (pastor). In the fourth chapter of Philippians it says:

> And you yourselves also know, Philippians, that at the first preaching of the gospel, after I departed from Macedonia, no church shared with me in the matter of giving and receiving but you alone; for even in Thessalonica you sent a gift more than once for my

needs (Philippians 4:15-16, NASB).

Givers realize that by giving to God's servants, they are actually giving to God. In Philippians 4:18, Paul says, "what you have sent [is] a fragrant aroma, an acceptable sacrifice, well-pleasing *to God*" (emphasis added).

Also, the trait of the motivation of Giver is found in the words "you sent a gift *more than once* for my needs" (emphasis added, 4:16). Everyone may give, occasionally, but the Giver makes giving a way of life. It is the *more-than-once* characteristic of giving that is one of the separators between the gift and the role of giving.

Notice too that Paul says that this church "shared with him in this ministry." Again, the Giver is *sharing* in the work by giving to the work. Those who simply give without the Giver Motivation may be *sharing* as well, but they are far less likely to see it that way. Perhaps it can be said, as indicated above, that the person who does not have the Giver Motivation but who gives financially is "helping" a ministry by his or her giving rather than *sharing* in that ministry. The Giver seems to have some aspect of "ownership" in the ministry to which he or she gives.

The Widow of Zarephath

There is a delightful and interesting story in First Kings about a widow in Zarephath who gave to the Lord via his servant Elijah. One aspect that makes this story and this woman so interesting is the passage that sets up the story. God says to the prophet: "Go at once to Zarephath of Sidon and stay there. I have commanded a widow in that place to supply you with food" (1 Kings 17:9). Though God tells Elijah that He has "commanded a widow in that place to supply" him with food, when the prophet approaches her, she seems to know nothing about this "command of the Lord." One would expect that when the prophet arrives the woman would say, "Oh, yes. I've been expecting you. God commanded me to supply you with food." However, rather than that, we read this:

> So he went to Zarephath. When he came to the town gate, a widow was there gathering sticks. He called to her and asked, "Would you bring me a little water in a jar so I may have a drink?" As she was going to get it, he called, "And bring me, please, a piece of bread." *"As surely as the LORD your God lives,"* she replied, *"I don't have any bread—only a handful of flour in a jar and a little oil in a jug. I am gathering a few sticks to take home and make a meal for myself and my son, that we may eat it—and die"* (emphasis added, 1 Kings 17:10-12).

If this woman had the "gift of giving," she seemed utterly unaware of it. In fact, Elijah had to tell her this:

> Don't be afraid. Go home and do as you have said. But first make a small cake of bread for me from what you have and bring it to me, and then make something for yourself and your son. For this is what the LORD, the God of Israel, says: "The jar of flour will not be used up and the jug of oil will not run dry until the day the LORD gives rain on the land" (1 Kings 17:13-14).

The prophet had to assure her that God was going to use her in a supernatural way—through her giving to the prophet. Who would deny that this was indeed a supernatural gift of giving? The fact that she did not know how God wanted to use her has been played out thousands of times since. God wants to use certain people, and they haven't got a clue as to their giftedness or ministry. Elijah assured her that God's hand was upon her, and he explained what His intentions were. In so doing, he "equipped her for the ministry" that God was about to give to her (see Ephesians 4:11-13).

Next, the Scripture says, "She went away and did as Elijah had told her. So there was food every day for Elijah and for the woman and her family" (1 Kings 17:15).

Givers cannot help but be blessed as well by the supply that God gives.

Remember, one aspect of Givers is that they seem to have enough for others and themselves. As they remain an open avenue (conduit) for the Lord's blessings to others, He continues to pour His blessings through them to others. At the same time, the Givers cannot help but be blessed as well by the supply that God gives.

Administrator

Joseph

A very good example of a person with the motivation of Administrator is found in the book of Genesis. Genesis 41 gives the account of Joseph interpreting the Egyptian Pharaoh's dreams. In this exchange between Joseph and Pharaoh, the Pharaoh perceives Joseph's administrative abilities and sets him up as his personal administrator. Administrators are good at defining long-range goals and can relate those goals to others, and Joseph is no exception. Joseph says to Pharaoh, speaking by divine revelation:

> Behold, seven years of great abundance are coming in all the land of Egypt; and after them seven years of famine will come, and all of the abundance will be forgotten in the land of Egypt; and the famine will ravage the land. . . . And now let Pharaoh look for a man discerning and wise, and set him over the land of Egypt (Genesis 41:29-30, 33 NASB).

After these words, Joseph went on to explain to Pharaoh exactly how to conduct business so as to save the people from the coming famine. Pharaoh replied:

> Since God has informed you of all this, there is no one so discerning and wise as you are. You shall be over my house, and according to your command all my people shall do homage; only in the throne I will be

greater than you . . . See I have set you over all the land of Egypt (Genesis 41:39-41, NASB).

Joseph coordinated the commerce of Egypt so well that in a few years he had gained great wealth for his employer: "Joseph bought all the land of Egypt for Pharaoh, for every Egyptian sold his field, because the famine was severe upon them. Thus, the land became Pharaoh's" (Genesis 47:20, NASB).

Nehemiah

One of the main motivations of the administrator is orderliness. The administrator is most uncomfortable when things are in disarray. Nehemiah was such a person.

One of the main motivations of the administrator is orderliness.

In Nehemiah 1:2-3, Nehemiah asked about the condition of those who survived the exile and about Jerusalem. The reply was that those who survived the exile were in great trouble and disgrace because the wall of Jerusalem was broken down. To this news Nehemiah replied: "When I heard these things I sat down and wept" (Nehemiah 1:4). Obviously Nehemiah wept for more than just the fact that the wall was in disarray; he wept also for the people, but the people were in great trouble and were disgraced because the wall of Jerusalem was broken down and the gates had been burned with fire (1:3).

Administrators are people of vision. Nehemiah had

assessed the problem and had devised a long-range plan to reach a common goal, the rebuilding of the wall.

Administrators also have the ability to know what tasks to delegate and which they should retain for themselves. Nehemiah delegated the rebuilding of the walls, and even then he had everything organized.

> From that day on, half of my men did the work, while the other half were equipped with spears, shields, bows and armor. The officers posted themselves behind all the people of Judah who were building the wall. Those who carried materials did their work with one hand and held a weapon in the other, and each of the builders wore his sword at his side as he worked. But the man who sounded the trumpet stayed with me (Nehemiah 4:16-18).

When one reads through the book of Nehemiah with an eye on Nehemiah's Administrative Motivation, it seems that neatness, order, goal objectives, and procedures to attain the goals are found in abundance throughout this book. Even in the last words of Nehemiah, his administrative characteristics (and thus motivation) are apparent:

> So I purified the priests and the Levites of everything foreign, and assigned them duties, each to his own task. I also made provision for contributions of wood at designated times, and for the firstfruits. Remember me with favor, O my God (Nehemiah 13:30-31).

Nehemiah's last words in the book, "Remember me with favor, O my God," seem to say that he had accomplished what it was that God had called him to do. Though Nehemiah may not have called it such, he had faithfully exercised his Motivational Gift, his inborn character of administration, for the glory of God and the benefit of those who survived the exile. And, having done so, he expected that God would remember him.

Mercy

Jesus

Jesus is an example of the motivation of Mercy. The Scripture says, "For we do not have a high priest who cannot sympathize with our weaknesses, but who has been tempted in all things as we are, yet without sin" (Hebrews 4:15 NASB). Notice that Jesus sympathizes with our weaknesses. The word sympathize in this text means "to suffer with another." Thus, Jesus is able to feel (sympathize with) what we feel. The person with the Mercy Motivation will be able to identify with and actually feel the misery or happiness of others. Jesus, then, as our high priest, identifies with our weaknesses and actually feels our pains. (That is not to imply that He is limited to our weaknesses, for He is neither weak nor limited.)

It was mercy and sympathy that moved Jesus to heal the sick.

It was mercy and sympathy that moved Jesus to heal the sick, Matthew 20:24, Mark 1:41; feed the hungry, Mark

6:34-42; cast out devils, Mark 9:22-27; and raise the dead, Luke 7:13-15.

Jesus is Our Example in All the Gifts

However, Jesus not only had the Motivational Gift of Mercy, He had all of the gifts. Thus, Jesus is our example in all of the Motivational Gifts.

He operated in the motivation of Prophet. He spoke the truth to all mankind not fearing man nor the reprisals of man.

He operated in the motivation of Server. He washed the feet of His disciples.

He operated in the motivation of Teacher. He studied the Scriptures and taught the disciples and others many truths of the Kingdom of God.

He operated in the motivation of Exhorter. He encouraged His disciples and others to grow in spiritual maturity.

He operated in the motivation of Giver. He gave Himself (and He is the *riches of heaven*) to benefit mankind, and the Kingdom of God.

He operated in the motivation of Administrator. He coordinated the activities of His disciples, and of His own life to reach the far-range goals that the Father had sent Him to accomplish.

Jesus' words, "I am among you as one who serves" (Luke 22:27c NASB) is the basis of His exercise of all of the gifts. Likewise, service through love should be the Christian's basis for the exercise of the gifts.

---

[1] S. M. Horton, *The Book of Acts* (Springfield, Mo.: Gospel Publishing House, 1981) p. 70.

[2] Ibid., p. 141.

[3] Ibid., p. 187.

Chapter 8

The Motivational Gifts in Ministry

An interesting point is discussed by Bill Gothard. The Greek word charisma is translated gifts in Romans 12:6, and the Greek word chara is translated as joy. Thus, both gifts and joy are from the same root word char. Therefore, the implication is that when one is operating in the charismata (gifts) that the Lord has given to him or her, a natural outcome of that operation will be personal chara (joy).[1]

It seems apparent that people experience joy when they are functioning in the gifts that God has given to them. While interviewing hundreds of people, I discovered that they found joy and fulfillment in their various jobs if they had occupations that allowed them to exercise their giftedness:

Some with the gift of Administrator were employed as administrators.

Some with the gift of Server were police officers, mechanics, and carpenters. As I recall, one wanted to open a *Bed and Breakfast*.

Some with the Motivation of Teacher were public-school teachers, analysts, and lawyers.

Others with the Mercy Motivation were working with physically and mentally challenged children and adults, some were medical personnel.

Still others who were gifted Exhorters were employed as state-licensed counselors and school counselors.

Even though these Christian people were in secular jobs, they found great joy in expressing the giftedness that God had given to them in their secular careers.[2]

Also, it was no surprise to find ministers who received great joy in functioning in their areas of giftedness within ministry. It is a tremendous personal blessing to discover one's gift and to operate in it, whether in ministry or a secular job. It is also a tremendous burden to constantly work outside of one's giftedness. I've met pastors who were doing aspects of ministry for which they were not gifted, and some of them were burned-out and exhibited no joy in their ministries.

Motivational Gifts for Everybody

The question often comes up: "Do only Christians have these gifts, or does everybody?" It is the premise of the *Motivational Gifts theory* that these particular gifts are inherent qualities. They are part of what the Psalmist David calls being fearfully and wonderfully made.

For you created my inmost being; you knit me together in my mother's womb. I praise you because I am fearfully and wonderfully made; your works are wonderful, I know that full well. My frame was not hidden from you when I was made in the secret place. When I was woven together in the depths of the earth, your eyes saw my unformed body. All the days ordained for me were written in your book before one of them came to be (Psalm 139:13-16).

Over the years, I have consistently received feedback indicating that people believed their particular Motivational Gifts had been with them all of their lives and not only after becoming Christians. I too believe that my particular Motivational Gift has been operative all of my life, i.e., before and after becoming a Christian. In fact, it was the analytical nature of my gift of Teacher (spurred on by the Holy Spirit) which caused me to investigate the claims of Christ and the evidences for the existence of God, which then, ultimately led me to faith in Christ.

With this premise in mind, that the Gifts are inherent, I agreed to teach a communications class to a group of people for a large corporation. The class was part of a job-enhancement program. I took my research material on the Motivational Gifts of Romans 12 and removed the spiritual jargon and proceeded to explain the truths concerning them.

I administered a modified version of the *Walston Gifts Indicator*—retitled the *Motivational Driver Indicator*—to the class to discover their "Motivational Drivers." I identified the characteristics of each of the motivations, and each person saw himself or herself in one of the Motivational Gifts. Most of the people in the class were not Christians, yet they also reported that they had always seen life through their particular "Motivational Driver," i.e., Motivational Gift.

Empirical evidence gathered over a long period of time by many researchers indicates that people are born with predisposed attitudes or personalities. In what appears to be a subtle but radical move from majority Christian opinion, Bittlinger asserts that God has given gifts to every human, both Christian and non-Christian. It is when man submits his life to God that his gifts are energized to be all that they were meant to be.[3]

This position of the innate quality of the Motivational Gifts does not imply that these gifts are anything less than supernatural. They are supernatural because God is the Giver. But, they are given to very natural creatures— humans. For example, if an unsaved person has a seemingly "natural" talent to express and communicate truth as a teacher, all of the glory goes to God because it was God who made the person and endowed that person with the ability to teach. Obviously this talent may be enhanced by the individual's hard work at cultivating the teaching ability, but the drive to be a teacher and the basic underlying ability is a God-given quality even if it is not being used for God's glory.

If human personality can be equated with the Motivational Gifts, which is the theory of the Motivational Gifts, then the fact of their inherent quality must be accepted. In *Unwrapping Your Spiritual Gifts*, David Allan Hubbard argues that the gifts that God bestows are a genetic inheritance, mixed with environment and training.[4]

So, it seems that while psychologists such as Jung and Isabel Briggs Myers were able to discover the truth that each person has a personality that is an inherent quality, it is all the more exciting and wondrous for the Christian to realize that it was God Himself who equipped or gifted each person with a unique personality type.

Also, since they are to be the stewards of God's gifts to them, it is the responsibility of all Christians to discover their giftedness and learn to employ it in some way for the edification of the Body of Christ. Furthermore, it is incumbent upon Christian leaders and pastors to help people discover and exercise their particular giftedness.

People are born with a predominant gift, and it remains the same throughout their lifetime. However, people mature in their gifts. Subsequently, one may notice a change in gift operation over the years, but this is not a change of gifts but of one's maturing in the gift one already has.

In bringing the subject of the inherent quality of the Motivational Gifts to a close, it is necessary to point out that neither the manifestations of the Spirit (1 Corinthians 12), nor the ministry gifts (Ephesians 4:11) are inherent gifts. Though all humans are born with a predisposition which reflects their God-given personality, only born-again believers may exercise one or more of the gifts in 1 Corinthians 12 or in Ephesians 4:11.

Fulfillment of the Gifts

Although non-Christians have these inherent Motivational Gifts, the gifts can only be *properly exercised* by *Christians* who are operating in their God-given function. Each gift, inherent or otherwise, is given by God and designed to edify and perfect the Body of Christ (Romans 12:2-5, Ephesians 4:16, 1 Corinthians 12:14-26). As all members in the Body of Christ function in their gifts, the Body finds its completeness.

The gifts can only be properly exercised by Christians who are operating in their God-given function.

Romans 12:4-5 states, "Just as each of us has one body with many members, and these members do not all have the same function, so in Christ we who are many form one body, and each member belongs to all the others." Though people may be "exercising" their Motivational Gift every day as a natural outflow of their particular personality, Christians are to use their God-given gifts to support and edify the Body of Christ:

> There should be no division in the body, but that the members should have the same care one for another. And if one member suffers, all the members suffer with it; if one member is honored, all the members rejoice with it. Now you are Christ's body, and individually members of it (1 Corinthians 12:25-27, NAS).

If members of the Body of Christ are not functioning in their particular gifts, they cannot be effective in supporting others of the Body of Christ. "Being fitted and held together by that which every joint supplies, according to the proper working of each individual part, causes the growth of the body for the building up of itself in love" (Ephesians 4:16, NAS). Peter says, "As each one has received a special gift, employ it in serving one another, as good stewards of the manifold grace of God" (1 Peter 4:10, NAS).

To the extent that a single Christian is not functioning in his or her gift, to that degree the Body of Christ is weakened. Therefore, these gifts, though they reside in every person saved and unsaved, have their proper function only when Christians are exercising them to fulfill God's will and edify the Body of Christ.

Achieving the Greatest Results

When pastors know their gifts and operate in them, they will generally have the greatest effectiveness with the least amount of weariness. Some pastors are caught in a ministerial trap of functioning outside their area of giftedness. For instance, if pastors who have the gift of Teaching are always comforting the bereaved, ministering to shut-ins, administrating church activities, counseling, or doing something else that is not within the scope of their Motivational Gifts, they will quickly suffer fatigue. Fatigue, also known as "burnout," is a complete exhaustion and depletion of emotional resources, enthusiasm, and energy. When this happens there is a great injustice perpetrated on the pastor and the church.

Pastors, teachers, prophets, administrators, *et al.*, need to be released to do the work that God has *enabled* them to do. Pastors must focus and do ministry in accordance with their giftedness. That is, they need to operate in the area of their gifts and callings. Functioning outside of one's giftedness will lead to the dreaded burnout.

That is not to imply, for example, that the Teacher-Motivated pastor will never minister to the shut-ins, the bereaved, or do counseling. But, if pastors (or others in ministry) *continuously* try to function outside the Motivations that God has given them, they will be easily wearied and less effective in their work for God.

Multiple Church Staffs and Motivational Gifts

Many larger churches have attempted to remedy the burnout problem by having several pastors on staff. Each pastor specializes in a certain aspect of ministry: a pastor of education, of visitation, of evangelism, and so on. This is a good *approach* to effectiveness in ministry. But even in this approach, the motivation of each pastor must be taken into account.

If on a multiple staff those with the Service Motivation are given the task of research and teaching, they will find themselves less effective and, eventually, exhausted. Or, if on a multiple staff those with the Prophet Motivation are assigned the ministry of pastoral care, they will be less effective than if they were proclaiming the truths of God. So, even though there may be multiple members on a church staff, individual giftedness and abilities must still be considered. If a church has a multiple staff and all or most of the staff are asked to function in an "office" or ministry outside their particular areas of giftedness, then there will still be "ministerial dysfunction" and burnout. Under these conditions, however, it will be on a larger scale.

Hiring a Multiple Staff

Too often in selecting a multiple staff, people are hired based on how close in personality they are to the senior pastor (or boss). Often, a senior pastor will be attracted to and hire others who have the same Personality Filter as himself. Since the two people have the same Personality Filter, they have immediate rapport. Since they have rapport, the pastor feels that this is a person with whom he can work, and so the individual is hired. If the pastor has the Teacher Motivation, and he is seeking someone to be the pastor of visitation, he should look for and hire someone who, perhaps, has the Mercy Motivation. Yet, because one of the interviewees also has the Teacher Motivation, and she and the pastor have an immediate "personality bonding," the pastor may hire her instead. In so doing, the pastor has placed a person in a ministry for which she is not innately nor spiritually qualified. Furthermore, the new hire will be stifled in ministry because she will not have the opportunity to function in her particular area of giftedness.

Therefore, even in a multiple staff, each person's Motivational Gift (psychological type) should be taken into account and matched with the appropriate ministry. The individuals on a multiple staff should be hired according to their giftedness and matched with *that aspect of ministry that will most release them to function in their God-given abilities and giftedness.*

Guilt in Ministry

Another problem that arises when people are placed into ministries that are outside their giftedness and abilities is that they may not truly enjoy their ministry. Guilt is often associated with being placed in a ministry for which one is not motivationally equipped to fulfill. Ministers may even function quite well (as a result of natural learning) in an area of ministry for which they are not suited. However, outward appearances notwithstanding, they will not enjoy their ministry. When this happens, the ministers may begin to think that there is something wrong with them. After all, shouldn't a minister thoroughly enjoy the ministry? It is not long before the minister may feel a burden of guilt for this secret disdain for "the ministry."

My Journey

I remember that early in my first pastorate, I didn't have a clue that God had given me a special gift and that I was to function in that gift for the betterment of the Body. Consequently, I attempted to do *all of the various ministries* in the church with equal energy. However, I soon discovered that I did not enjoy hospital or home visitations. I also felt that my time as a minister could be better spent locked away in research for next week's sermons and lectures rather than supporting a certain family by attending their son's little-league baseball game. But, in doing all of these "other ministries," I began to develop feelings of resentment toward these other aspects of "ministry."

These feelings of resentment made me feel guilty and inadequate. It wasn't until I came to understand the Motivational Gifts theory (as well as having formally studied psychological personality types later in college) that I began to understand that my gift was that of a Teacher, and not Mercy and Server. No wonder I was not enjoying these other aspects of ministry. God had not equipped me to function therein.

Far from feeling guilty, I began to understand the young shepherd David when *he refused to wear Saul's armor*. In essence, he was saying to Saul, *"You fight your giants your way, and I will fight my giants in the manner that God has gifted me."* Likewise, I began to realize that

God had gifted me as a Teacher, and that was my area of strength. As the pastor of a very small church at that time, I still had to do all of the many and various aspects of ministry, but I no longer *felt guilty* for not enjoying them as much as I enjoyed leading Bible studies and doing theological research.

The concept of discovering one's particular area of giftedness and then functioning in that area is not a self-centered twist on the truth of the gospel. For when Christians discover their particular gifts and are allowed to function in them, it not only helps that person, but it also edifies the Body of Christ (Romans 12:4-8, 1 Corinthians 12:7-31, Ephesians 4:12-16). Bryant reports that a Lutheran church in Detroit grew from 150 in Sunday school to 800; the budget grew from $150,000 to $800,000; and the main worship service grew from 400 to over 1000 over a five-year period. When asked how this tremendous growth took place the pastor explained that the church had grown due to the fact that they had begun requiring all members to discover and practice their spiritual gifts.[5]

The Body of Christ will be edified as Christians search for, discover, and function in their spiritual gifts. It is not human-centeredness to attempt to place Christians in ministries for which they are equipped and not to place them in ministries for which they are not equipped. It is, rather, equipping the saints for the work of ministry (Eph. 4:11-12).

The Small Church Curse

Often in smaller churches both the pastor and

congregation suffer. The smaller church rarely has the finances to hire more than one pastor. Thus, the one pastor ends up being a sort of "spiritual jack-of-all-trades." The pastor endeavors to do all things necessary for the congregation. In so doing he functions outside his Motivational Gift a majority of the time. In this setting, it is not long before he tires and becomes too worn-out to be proficient in any area. No individual can be a skilled worker in all areas.

The congregation also suffers because the pastor cannot meet all the needs of all the people. The pastor has tried to do everything but accomplishes very little of anything. On Sundays he is too far spent to feed the people "spiritual meat" but only the milk of the Word. Many pastors are called on by the church to do everything except that which they are specifically equipped to do. Peter says, "As each one has received a special gift, employ *it* in serving one another, as good stewards of the manifold grace of God" (emphasis added, 1 Peter 4:10, NAS). Having been the pastor of a small church, I understand the frustration of trying to be "all things to all people." Pastors and other ministers need to be released to do the work that they are best equipped to do.

A Dynamic Ministry Context

A dynamic ministry context could be created by bringing together a group of ministers, at least seven, in one church who represented *each* of the seven Motivational Gifts. Not all of these people would have to be paid staff, but they could be the deacons or elders that would give themselves to the work of the ministry. This would release pastors to do their work more efficiently. Usually within each church all the Motivational Gifts are represented within the laity, but to get people to do the work of the ministry is another problem.

Too often laypeople would never think of going to the hospital to visit the sick or do some other type of ministry because that is seen as the "pastor's job." Thus, the devil frustrates the work of the kingdom by keeping people ignorant of their gifts and by keeping those who do know what their gifts are from functioning in them. However, when people discover that they have in fact been gifted by God to do certain aspects of ministry, their attitudes change and they begin to see themselves as *participants in ministry* instead of mere spectators.

As Christians begin to learn what their gifts are, they will begin to see that they can be used in the work of the Lord. And, as they do the work that they are called to do, this will release the leadership and others to do the work that they are called to do. By all Christians functioning in their particular gifts and thereby allowing the church leadership time and opportunity to function in the areas of giftedness for which they are enabled, Christians can frustrate the work of the devil.

All Christians are to Minister

A common mistake that laypeople make is thinking that only the pastor can do the work of the ministry. But the work of the ministry is to be done by all Christians. This is a truth taught in the Word of God (Ephesians 4:12) that has been largely lost in the Church today. Oh, there's plenty of talk about laypeople being equipped for ministry, but there is relatively little action to go along with all of the talk. One of the main reasons that "common" Christians do not think they can do the work of the ministry is because they are unaware that God has endowed them with gifts to enable them to minister. God gave the Five-fold[6] gifts of Ephesians 4:11 to the church "to prepare God's people for works of service" (Ephesians 4:12). This means, simply, that pastors and other leaders in the church are *responsible* to teach Christians how to function in their God-given gifts.

For example, the person with the Mercy Motivation would be helpful in ministering to shut-ins and others at retirement homes, and much more.

The person with the Teaching Motivation would be a great asset in home Bible studies or Sunday school.

The person with the Administration Motivation would be valuable in organizing outings, retreats, and other meetings for the church.

The person with the Server Motivation could lead a troupe of laborers to minister to the physical needs of members in the church. I once heard of a church where several people were involved in the "service" ministry of the church. Their phone numbers were made available to the congregation, and when *Sister Widow's* sink got stopped up, she was able to call someone on that list. When a church member's car broke down, someone on the list was able to meet the person and help fix the car. The list goes on and on. The needs within the local church are limitless, but the variations of the exercise of the gifts are limitless as well.

When all the individuals of the Body begin to do the work of the ministry in the various areas for which they are gifted, Christ's Body will then begin to function as it should. The purpose of the saints doing the work of the ministry, says Paul, is "so that the Body of Christ may be built up" (Ephesians 4:12). Functioning in one's gift as a work of ministry is meant to be an ongoing work "until we all reach unity in the faith and in the knowledge of the Son of God and become mature, attaining to the whole measure of the fullness of Christ" (Ephesians 4:13). Every Christian has a tremendous ministry. Discovering and functioning in one's Motivational Gift will allow individuals the fulfillment of that ministry.

---

[1] Bill Gothard, *How To Understand Spiritual Gifts* (Oak Brook, Il.: Institute in Basic Life Principles, 1981), p. 50.

[2] I conducted some interviews with various people who were participants in lectures that I gave on the Motivational Gifts/ Psychological Types theory.

[3] Arnold Bittlinger, *Gifts and Ministries* (Grand Rapids, Mi.: Eerdmans Publishing Co., 1973), p. 13.

[4] David Allen Hubbard, *Unwrapping Your Spiritual Gifts* (Waco, Tx.: Word Books, 1985), pp. 107-111.

[5] Ibid., p. 55. I am not implying that anyone who mechanically employs the same requirements of discovering and exercising gifts in any given church will necessarily have the same results. A key point, just to name one, is the fact that Detroit has a large population from which to draw for numerical growth. Thus, I am not advocating a blind repetition of this church's efforts *for the purpose of* numerical growth. However, it is my belief that all churches should encourage the discovery and function of the gifts of the Spirit among the

laypeople. For part of equipping the saints to do the work of ministry is to help them discover their gifts (1 Timothy 4:11-16). Effectiveness in ministry is part of the natural outgrowth of the exercise of giftedness.

6 The reference to the gifts in Ephesians as "Five-fold" reflects my own theological bias. It is my opinion that there are five and not four gifts listed in this passage. See also W. A. Criswell *The Baptism, Filling & Gifts of the Holy Spirit* (Grand Rapids, Mi.: Zondervan Publishing House, 1973), p. 59.; Kenneth Cain Kinghorn, *Gifts of the Spirit* (Nashville, Tn.: Abingdon Press, 1976), p. 43.; W. Harold Mare, "1 Corinthians," in *The Expositor's Bible Commentary*, gn. ed. Frank E. Gaebele, vol. 10, (Grand Rapids, Mi.: Zondervan Publishing House, 1976), p. 266.

Chapter 9

Do Opposites Attract? A Prevailing Myth in Our Culture

The old saying that "opposites attract" is an old saw whose time to die has come. In reality, people are more often attracted to others with qualities that are the same as or similar to what they have. Statistically, people who are the same (or similar) are attracted to each other far more often than opposites are.

Many people quantitatively overstate the fact that "opposites attract" by claiming or implying that "opposites *more often than not* attract." Some have concluded that just because people marry others who have motivational gifts (or personalities) that are different from their own, they have thus married others who are *opposite* from themselves. This conclusion is simply unsubstantiated and is based solely on an arbitrary and inaccurate understanding of the various differences and similarities of the Motivational Gifts (and personality types).

In looking at some of the literature on this topic of opposites attracting one another, I discovered that some less-than-qualified "researchers" have attempted to make their subjects fit into one of two extremes: either the gifts of the married couples were exactly the same, or, consequently, they were diametrically opposing gifts. They allowed for only two outcomes: (1) People are opposites or (2) People are exactly the same. However, they left out the possibility of a third outcome: (3) People are *similar.*

These researchers "graded" the gifts (and personality types) on "the pendulum" rather than on "a continuum." It is, however, more accurate to "grade" the various responses of couples on a continuum, *"progressive scale."* Thus, at one end of the scale are those who are exactly the same, and on the other end of the scale are those who are exact opposites. And, throughout the scale between the two extremes is a unity, non-unity gradation. Thus, even though a couple may not have the exact same gifts nor the exact opposite gifts, they may in fact be very similar or quite dissimilar.

Keirsey and Bates point out that their twenty years of research has indicated that opposites do attract each other with high frequency.[1] Their statement "with high frequency" is a good qualifier. For while it is true that some people are attracted to and marry their opposites, this is not always the case, nor is it almost always the case.

Isabel Briggs Myers has pointed out that her research of various personality types indicated that couples marry their opposite types less frequently than their similar types. Thus, people more often marry others who are similar to themselves than those who are opposite from themselves.[2] Not only that, but Myers' research also shows that people marry their *exact same type* more often than their *exact opposite type* by a margin of more than two to one! Nine percent of these people married others with the exact same psychological types *while only four percent married their exact opposites*. An overwhelmingly large percentage (68%) of those interviewed by Isabel Briggs Myers married others who were similar to themselves.

People more often marry others who are similar to themselves than those who are opposite from themselves.

Also, research studies conducted by the Center for

Applications of Psychological Type reveal that from a random assortment of 1,142 psychological types, people are more likely to marry others with the exact same type as themselves far more frequently than an exact opposite type.[3] In fact, ten percent of those studied had married others with the same psychological type whereas only six percent married others who were their opposites. And, 66% of the 1,142 people married others who were similar to themselves.

Then, from a decidedly Christian perspective, Stephen Grunlan points out that Dennis Orthner discovered that the majority of research indicates that mate selection is based on similarities, not opposites.[4] In confirmation of the findings of these researchers, I discovered that of a random assortment of 56 couples 20 of them married their opposites while 36 of them married someone who was similar to or the same as themselves. The similar/same couples outnumbered the opposite couples nearly two to one. The conclusion of this research is that *people who are similar are far more likely to become attracted to and marry one another than people who are opposites.*

Nevertheless, it seems that the popular myth that opposites attract more frequently than similar personalities is ingrained into our culture. As has been shown by the research of Isabel Briggs Myers, the Center for Applications of Psychological Type, Stephen Grunlan, and by my own research, those with the *same* personalities and motivational gifts marry with more frequency (about 2 to 1) than do opposites. And, those with similar (but not exactly the same) personalities marry with far more frequency (about 10 to 1) than do opposites. Thus, the empirical data indicate a serious flaw in the "opposites-attract theory." It is clear that the idea that "opposites *usually* attract" is simply wrong.

Opposites and Similarities in the Motivational Gifts

The various Motivational Gifts can be seen as opposites or similar according to their various characteristics. Mercy and Prophet would seem to be opposites because Mercy is concerned about the emotional status of a person in sin. Contrariwise, the Prophet is likely to preach a strong message of repentance to such a person with little or no regard for the individual's emotional status. Yet, other gifts have some similar characteristics. However, and this is somewhat surprising, some people seem to have both prophet and mercy as part of their PAT-Mix.

Both of the Motivational Gifts of Prophet and Teacher have the characteristic of being very "matter of fact." Both the Prophet and Teacher regard truth as more valuable than emotions. Therefore, the Prophet and Teacher would not be regarded as opposites; however, neither would they be considered identical. It is quite apparent, however, that they are more similar than dissimilar. Likewise, the Administrator and Teacher may also be considered quite similar. Both have the characteristics of being logical and analytical. Since the WGI gauges the response of each individual on all seven Motivational Gifts, I was able to make some conclusions as to the sameness, similarity, and oppositeness of the couples polled.

For instance, when considering a couple whose primary

gifts are Administrator (his) and Service (hers) (two gifts with similar characteristics), it immediately appears that the couple would be similar. These preliminary similarities notwithstanding, if Mr. Administrator had Prophet as his auxiliary gift, and Mrs. Service had Mercy as her auxiliary gift, they would in fact end up being opposites, at least on a *relative* scale—and all of this material is *relative* because what we know about the Motivational Gifts is limited at best. However, if a couple's primary gifts were Administrator (his) and Service (hers), and Mr. Administrator had Prophet as his auxiliary gift, and Mrs. Service also had Prophet as her auxiliary gift, they would in fact end up being the same, at least on a *relative* scale.

Furthermore, the five remaining gifts must be considered when gauging the sameness, similarity, and oppositeness between couples. For instance a husband may have the primary gift of Teacher and auxiliary gift of Exhorter. Then further down the line, the other five gifts may have come out in the order of Prophet, Server, Giver, Administrator, and Mercy. The wife may have as her primary and auxiliary gifts Administrator and Exhorter (the same auxiliary as the husband). At first glance, when considering only the first two gifts (husband is Teacher-Exhorter and the Wife is Administrator-Exhorter) it appears that these two are quite similar because they both have the same auxiliary gift and because Teacher and Administrator are similar in some characteristics. However, her remaining gifts may be in "opposite" order from his. For example, further down the line, her other listings may have come out in the order of Mercy, Giver, Server, Prophet, and Teacher. So the order would look like this:

HIS		HERS
Primary: Teacher	<—— similar ——>	Primary: Administrator
Auxiliary: Exhorter	<—— same ——>	Auxiliary: Exhorter

==

Prophet	<—— opposite ——>	Mercy
Server		Giver
Giver		Server
Mercy		Prophet
Administrator		Teacher

==

Thus, the only gift that the two spouses have in common is Exhorter. However, with the other gifts differing so widely, the common gift of Exhorter would not function in the same way for the husband as for the wife. The husband with his tertiary gift of Prophet would most likely taint the common gift of Exhorter to such a degree that it would bear little resemblance to his wife's auxiliary gift of Exhortation which is acted upon by her tertiary gift of Mercy. The remaining four gifts may also be taken into consideration as well, if not from a positive expression, at least from a negative one.

In other words, if a person's last gift on the continuum scale is Mercy, it may not affect the primary, auxiliary, or tertiary gifts in a positive sense. However, it may affect them negatively in that the gift of Mercy is most likely rarely employed, and thus none of the first three gifts are tainted by Mercy. Whereas if a person has Mercy as his fourth gift, it will *more often affect* the first three, given the proper circumstances.

All Motivational Gifts should be considered when gauging giftedness and spousal similarities. Since the

Bible has commanded each Christian to function in all seven gifts when the circumstances call for it (this will be discussed in detail below), we must conclude that all seven gifts have an effect in one way or another on the primary and auxiliary gifts. No person exercises his primary gift in a vacuum. Many things either help or hinder the expression of one's giftedness, i.e., God-given personality.

A Motivational-Gifts Knowledge in Counseling

As much as 30% to 40% of married couples will have dissimilar Motivational Gifts, thus, differing Personality Filters. It should also be pointed out that many people (perhaps as much as 80%) did not marry others with their exact same primary gifts. So, even though they may be similar, their differences are often wide enough to be a source of conflict in marriage. Therefore, while it is incorrect to say that *opposites usually attract*, it is fair to say that those who are *different* (not exact opposites) do often attract.

Some couples are opposites and more are dissimilar. Since this is true, it is imperative for Christian pastors and counselors to understand and implement the Motivational Gifts theory in counseling.

I once had an extensive counseling relationship with a husband and wife who were opposites from one another. The husband had the Motivational Gift of Prophet; his personality was very direct and to the point. Her Motivational Gift was Mercy. Her personality was very sensitive and compassionate. Next, the remaining gifts as indicated by the WGI showed that they were in opposition to one another.

At first, what attracted him to her was her compassion toward him, to others, and her overall tenderness. However, later in their marriage, he began to see her sensitivity as a weakness. In a counseling session the husband complained, "She never says what she feels; she is always afraid of hurting someone's feelings!"

And, at first she had been attracted to him because of his self-assuredness, and his ability to "tell it like it is," as she put it. But later she began to see his self-assuredness as arrogance and pride, and his "telling it like it is" as nothing more than boorish behavior.

The problem in their marriage did not stop with a simple recognition of the differences. Each person seemed bent on changing the other person. Each wanted the other to be more like himself or herself.

Lovers not Pygmalion

In Greek mythology, Pygmalion was a sculptor who fell in love with a statue of a woman that he had carved, and which Aphrodite brought to life as Galatea. Too often spouses act like sculptors rather than lovers.

Do couples who are opposites or relative opposites have a good chance of being successful in their marriage? Keirsey and Bates accurately conclude that couples who are opposites may succeed in their marriage as long as they resist the seemingly innate impulse to change their spouses. They state that couples must not attempt to sculpt their spouses into being someone they are not. They say that some people seemingly construe the marriage license into a sculptor's license, "giving each spouse the warrant to chisel away until the other becomes the spit and image of the sculptor. Consider the supreme irony were each spouse successful!"[5] The supreme irony is, of course, that the two would be exact opposites once again.

When people attempt to sculpt their spouses and remake them into something they are not, it sends the message that they are not accepted for who they are. It is impossible to change another individual into the likeness of oneself, but it is the *attempt* to sculpt and the *message* sent that does great damage to the marriage union. Keirsey and Bates explain that when this sculpting process goes on in a marriage, it shows a lack of appreciation of the very characteristics which were the cause of the initial attraction.[6] The Prophet-Mercy couple mentioned above had been attracted to each other even though they were opposites. They later complained of the very characteristics which at first attracted them to each other. They were both attempting to sculpt the other.

This is where the Christian counselor comes in. If this couple could only recognize that the characteristics of each spouse are part of the make up of their God-given personalities, i.e., Motivational Gifts, then perhaps they would be better able to understand and accept one another. *Furthermore*, to attempt to undo or change another person's Motivational Gift (personality type) is actually an attempt to undo or change *the very work of God*. For "We have different gifts, according to the grace given to us" (Romans 12:6).

Summary

Since there are those who become attracted to and marry their opposites, and there is even a greater number of folks who marry their "dissimilars," the need for a proper understanding of the Motivational Gifts among couples is quite necessary. Furthermore, pastors and counselors would benefit greatly by having an understanding of and the ability to identify the various Motivational Gifts.

When spouses are repulsed by what it was that first attracted them to each other, their marriage is headed for disaster. Each must learn what the other's Motivational Gift and Personality Filter is and accept each other as is. This takes the pressure off a person from trying to be someone that he or she is not. It also takes the pressure off the person who thinks he or she should be the other's sculptor. It is better to be oneself, as God designed, and let others be themselves too. This goes beyond the social bond of marriage and into the other social relationships we all have everyday. Acceptance, not alteration, is the key to unity on the job, in the ministry, or in the marriage.

All this is not to say that a person's negative, immature, or destructive traits are to be accepted as if they too are gifts from God. There are many negative traits that actually are bad and need to be corrected. Certainly abusive people cannot claim, "God made me this way." However, aside from these (and other) negative characteristics, people should not be asked to give up being who and what they are.

Each individual Christian is a part of the Body of Christ, and each has a different function. The eye does not feel, the hand does not smell, and the mouth does not hear. Every part of the Body of Christ, lacking no individual, is necessary for the whole of the Body of Christ to function properly.

Once you know what your particular Motivational Gift is, you can begin to smooth out your own negative traits. Also, you can learn to function with others who have differing Personality Filters than you do.

---

[1] David Keirsey and Marilyn Bates, *Please Understand Me* (Del Mar, Ca.: Prometheus Nemesis Book Company, 1984), p. 67.

[2] Isabel Briggs Myers and Mary H. McCaulley, *A Guide to the Development and Use of the Myers-Briggs Type Indicator* (Palo Alto, Ca.: Consulting Psychologists Press Inc., 1988), p. 71.

[3] Ibid.

[4] As quoted in Stephen A. Grunlan, *Marriage and the Family* (Grand Rapids, Mi.: Zondervan Publishing House, 1984), pp. 84-85.

[5] Keirsey and Bates, p. 68.

[6] Ibid.

Chapter 10

The
Walston Gifts Indicator:
Determining Your
Motivational Gifts

This chapter introduces the Walston Gifts Indicator (WGI), which will help you discover your particular Motivational Gift(s). I have administered WGI to several hundred people including more than one-hundred children (under eighteen).

A Word of Caution

While I believe that the Motivational Gifts are apparent in children, one must take *great care* in "identifying" a child's personality type. People can do more damage than good if they misidentify a child's personality type and then set out to nurture that particular type. I am aware that there are a few pop-treatments of helping children discover their motivational giftedness though various tests and attitude indictors. However, if the personality type that is identified for a child is not the correct one, he or she may grow up with the unnecessary burden of trying to be something or someone he or she is not. And, this can have far-reaching and devastating results.

Identifying children's personality types by asking them to gauge how they "feel" or what they "believe" about the various questions found in these types of indicators is itself a nebulous and unscientific task. Children will too often score the questions depending on several factors:

(1) how they *happen to be feeling that day, or that hour.*
(2) how they *think their parents* would want them to score it.

(3) how they think *their best friend* will score it.

(4) how they *wish they were* rather than how they actually are.

Therefore, as the author of this particular indicator, I would suggest that this tool—if used at all—*not* be the only one used when attempting to discover the personality-type or Motivational Gift of a child. This challenge belongs in the hands of those who are specifically trained in child psychology, preferably, a Christian child psychologist.

When I administered a modified version of this indicator to children, I would never state emphatically what their "gifts" were. Rather, I would simply tell them what all of the Motivational Gifts were, and I would tell them that it *appeared that they lean in certain directions*.

Furthermore, I also identified their top three gifts without putting them in a hierarchical order.

Last, I did not let them keep their written outcomes. Letting them know that God had given them gifts and that they were already able to begin to see their leanings was enough information for them. The fact that they were gifted seemed to be sufficient encouragement for them. Thus, as they grow and mature, they will be conscious of the fact that they have a particular and unique personality that God had given to them as His gift to them.

Process

Any person may self-administer and score the WGI by following the directions below. You do not need a description of the gifts before you can discover your gift(s).

You have been operating, to one degree or another, in your gift your entire lifetime. Thus, there only needs to be an identification of certain personality traits (or gift characteristics) to discover your Motivational Gift.

The WGI is a self-assessment tool that I developed in an effort to help Christians discover their Motivational Gifts. This particular assessment has been helpful and accurate in assisting hundreds of people in the discovery of their Motivational Gifts.

Not a Test

Please note that even though the WGI may look suspiciously like a test, *it is not a test*. There are no right or wrong responses to the WGI. Rather, it is simply a means by which individuals can recognize their personality traits and classify them within one (or more) of the seven Motivational Gifts.

Also, individual scores have *no relationship* to another person's scores. Therefore, you must write the answer that best fits you, and when you see your personal scores, do not "gauge" your score against the score of anyone else.

When answering the questions, you must be *totally* honest with yourself and with the Indicator. Without total honesty reflected in the scores one gives on the self report, the end result will be inadequate and incorrect.

Determining Your Motivational Gift Through the Walston Gifts Indicator

Directions

There are no "right" or "wrong" answers to the *Walston Gifts Indicator*. The answers you give will serve to indicate which of the seven Motivational Gifts you prefer to function in, in your daily life. God has placed the characteristics of one (or more) of the Motivational Gifts in every person. A knowledge of your particular gift will help you understand why you view things, operate, and function the way you do.

Answering the Identification Statements

Carefully read and evaluate each statement. Indicate your answers on the Answer Sheet by giving each statement a number value to indicate how closely you identify with the statement, or how true the statement is concerning you. *Be sure to place your answers on the correct corresponding blank space provided.* You must evaluate and answer *all* of the identification statements.

Explanation of Number Values

If you absolutely *do not* identify with the statement, or if the statement is never true of you, put a "0" in the blank space provided. If you identify with the statement only seldom to sometimes, place a "1" in the blank. If you think the statement is usually or often true of you, place a "2" in the blank. If the statement is almost always true of you and/or you positively *do* identify with the statement, put a "3" in the blank provided. Again, here is how to score your answers: **Never = 0, Seldom to Sometimes = 1, Usually or Often = 2, Almost Always = 3.**

Please read over these number values again and become familiar with them before you begin evaluating the statements.

Answer Sheet
for Identification Statements

Never = 0   Seldom to Sometimes = 1
Usually to Often = 2   Almost Always = 3

WORK ACROSS – – – – – – –>

1 ____   2 ____   3 ____   4 ____   5 ____   6 ____   7 ____

8 ____   9 ____   10____   11____   12____   13____   14____

15____   16____   17____   18____   19____   20____   21____

22____   23____   24____   25____   26____   27____   28____

29____   30____   31____   32____   33____   34____   35____

36____   37____   38____   39____   40____   41____   42____

43____   44____   45____   46____   47____   48____   49____

50____   51____   52____   53____   54____   55____   56____

57____   58____   59____   60____   61____   62____   63____

64____   65____   66____   67____   68____   69____   70____

71____   72____   73____   74____   75____   76____   77____

78____   79____   80____   81____   82____   83____   84____

85____   86____   87____   88____   89____   90____   91____

92____   93____   94____   95____   96____   97____   98____

WORK ACROSS – – – – – – –>

Never = 0   Seldom to Sometimes = 1
Usually to Often = 2   Almost Always = 3

Directions for the Identification Statements

If possible, find a quiet place where you can relax while answering these questions. Carefully read and give a number value to each statement below. Mark your answers on the answer sheet above. Indicate how closely you identify with the statement or how true the statement is for you. Be sure to place your answers on the *correct corresponding blank space provided*. It is necessary that you evaluate and answer *all* of the statements.

As you assess these statements, you must be honest with yourself and with your evaluations. If a statement indicates a quality that you think is admirable but you realize that you do not have that quality, then answer with a number value that best reflects that fact. In a self-assessment such as this, an accurate outcome (the correct indication of your particular gift) can only be obtained by accuracy in your answers.

Evaluate the following identification statements with the Number Values:

Never = 0   Seldom to Sometimes = 1
Usually to Often = 2   Almost Always = 3

Identification Statements

1. I enjoy expressing God's truths verbally.

2. I demonstrate my love by meeting the *practical* needs of others.

3. I enjoy involving myself in *detailed* study of the Bible.

4. When I go through hard times or suffering, I do not mind because I know it will bring me to new levels of spiritual maturity.

5. I enjoy giving my personal things to help someone's ministry.

6. I have the ability to organize tasks within a job or ministry so as to produce efficiency.

7. I share deeply in other people's sadness.

8. It is easy to detect if a person is a true Christian because *true* Christians show forth their Christianity by the outward evidences of a godly lifestyle.

9. I like manual projects. I enjoy using my hands in work (could be anything from setting tables to mechanics).

10. Once I believe something, it takes nothing less than solid facts to change my mind. An emotional appeal will not change my mind.

11. When people come to me for advice, I have the *ability* to help and encourage them.

12. When I give money or things to the Lord's work, I do it cheerfully.

13. I enjoy coordinating (or administrating) activities.

14. I have a strong desire to comfort and show mercy to people with emotional problems.

15. I don't "beat around the bush" when I talk to people. I just *tell it like it is.*

16. As long as I am helping others, I can work long hours with very little need of rest.

17. I do not believe something just because the pastor, evangelist, or someone else has said it. I investigate and validate truth for myself.

18. I have the ability to lay out detailed steps of action for others so they can reach new levels of spiritual maturity.

19. I have a *tender heart* and give to almost anyone who has a need.

20. I have the ability to survey a task and understand the total scope of a job.

21. I have a great deal of sympathy for people in emotional distress.

22. I have delivered messages of judgment and repentance which I believe have come from God. (Not necessarily in the preaching mode, but perhaps just talking with someone.)

23. If I am called upon to help someone with a physical need, I do it cheerfully, even if my part seems small and insignificant.

24. I am meticulous in my study of the Bible or other things I may be researching; each detail is important.

25. I have the ability to draw answers from the Bible for human affliction and suffering (for individuals, not world problems).

26. I *enjoy* giving financial help to people and ministries, and I often do it anonymously.

27. I have the ability to administrate, organize, and facilitate projects to accomplish a group goal.

28. I try to help people overcome their emotional distress *as soon as possible.*

29. I seem to have the ability to discern, or "see through," people's motives.

30. I am deeply touched by the practical and physical needs of others.

31. I place an emphasis on the preciseness and accuracy of words.

32. I am *motivated* to lead Christians to higher levels of spiritual maturity.

33. I believe that I could adjust to a lower standard of living for the purpose of benefiting God's work financially.

34. I would rather organize a meeting than be the speaker of a meeting.

35. I avoid hurting people's feelings at almost all costs.

36. I see things as either right or wrong, black or white; there are no gray or neutral areas.

37. I am alert to and I help meet the *practical* needs of others.

38. I like to listen to systematic teaching laid out in a clear, orderly fashion, even if the lecturer is not a great speaker.

39. My motto is "Things are going to get better." (The idea, not the exact words.)

40. I budget my finances so that I can give generously to the Lord's work.

41. I enjoy being responsible for the organization of a meeting.

42. I have been told that I am, "too emotional."

43. I am an open, honest, realistic, and practical person.

44. I believe people should be more willing to help others with their practical and physical everyday needs.

45. When someone tells me something that I am not sure is true, I check up on it by researching the facts.

46. If a person has gone through a bad experience, I advise him or her to learn from the experience and to look forward to the future.

47. When I give to a person or ministry, I feel like I am sharing a part of myself.

48. When I organize a party or other functions, I like to arrange everything in advance.

49. I enjoy spending time with shut-in people because I know that it is a comfort for them to have someone around during times of suffering.

50. I often tell people to repent or straighten up if their

lifestyle is not pleasing to God.

51. I have a wide range of physical abilities (or talents), kind of a jack-of-all-trades.

52. When someone says that he has a "revelation" from God, his "revelation" absolutely must coincide with the Bible, or I simply dismiss it.

53. I am a very positive and "up" sort of person, always seeing the future as better days ahead.

54. I believe that Christians are to tithe and give offerings beyond the tithe.

55. I can set goals for the future and clearly communicate these goals.

56. When I counsel someone who has been hurt, I let my emotions guide the counseling more than my logic.

57. I hold *strong* moral convictions based upon my judgments of right and wrong.

58. Actions speak louder than words, so if someone has something physical that needs to be fixed, I won't just say I care, I'll help fix it.

59. Jesus commands us to love God with our minds as well as our hearts. Thus, He wants us to be logical, thinking people.

60. I often tell people something like, "You'll do better next time," or, "You are going to be a better person for having gone through this situation."

61. Even though I may get money from my job, I am *very* aware that God is truly the source of my supply.

62. If I am in a situation with a group of people where something has to be accomplished but no one seems to be in charge, I will assume the leadership and coordinate the group to accomplish the task.

63. When I walk into a room where there is an atmosphere of distress, I perceive the distress immediately.

64. Telling the truth is more important than being considerate of people's feelings.

65. In service for God, I would like to help by doing manual tasks and thereby free up the pastor to be able to do what he does best.

66. My beliefs are substantiated by a *personal knowledge of the Bible*, and not just what I've been told by others.

67. I encourage people by explaining to them ways they can grow and mature.

68. I believe people should give their finances more freely to those in need.

69. I make a list of the things I need before going shopping. I *often* make lists, whether for things I need to buy or things I need to do.

70. If necessary, I will comfort and show mercy to others even if by doing so I put myself in danger.

71. I believe the church should be just as concerned about getting society on the straight path as it is about helping individuals.

72. Sometimes I get myself too involved with helping others because I have a hard time saying "no" to people in need.

73. If I were shown that what I believe is wrong, even if I didn't like it emotionally, I would change my beliefs to fit the facts.

74. I love to lift up, strengthen, and encourage others. Therefore I enjoy spending much time counseling people.

75. I enjoy giving money or other material assets to those in need.

76. I detest disorganization.

77. I don't just say I feel sorry for someone; I display my sympathy by acts of kindness.

78. I make quick moral judgments about things I see or hear, and then I make my judgments known by talking openly about them.

79. I am a very hospitable person, and I enjoy waiting on people as their host.

80. If I am going to listen to someone preach or lecture, I like to know what kind of education, or teaching credentials, he/she has.

81. I have the ability to help people turn failures and persecution into stepping stones to spiritual growth.

82. God always supplies me with enough finances and material things so I can continue to give to others in need.

83. I prefer to follow a schedule rather than being open-ended.

84. I have the ability to show love to people others call the "unlovely."

85. I want people to say exactly what they mean, without "beating around the bush."

86. I tend to disregard my own health and comfort in an effort to serve others.

87. I place a strong emphasis on accuracy when reporting

on a situation or incident.

88. I am a creative person, always seeing new possibilities to situations.

89. I believe that God "tests" my faithfulness by the way I handle money.

90. I can effectively coordinate projects and activities so as to successfully accomplish a task within the given time-frame (by due date).

91. I am a person of deep feelings, and I make decisions more often based on my feelings rather than on logical analysis.

92. When I believe something is morally right, I openly show my commitment to it no matter who opposes me.

93. I enjoy helping people with physical needs (could be such things as helping clean someone's house or fix their car).

94. When listening to a sermon or lecture, I notice and remember factual details more than most people do.

95. I am able to tell what spiritual level people are at and communicate with them on their level.

96. I see financial needs of people and ministries which others seem to overlook.

97. When I take a trip or vacation, I like to plan out every detail so that everything is in order.

98. Though I am concerned about people's physical needs, people's emotional needs are more important to me.

How to Score the WGI

After you have answered all the questions and filled in all the spaces with the appropriate number values, you can score the *Indicator* by adding the numbers vertically (down each column) as demonstrated below. The columns are in the same order as the gifts listed in Romans 12.

This sample below starts with question number 50 so as to save space. You, of course, will add all of your answers from one to ninety-eight.

Identification Statements

Never = 0 Seldom to Sometimes = 1 Usually to Often = 2
Almost Always = 3

Add **down** each column and place your scores on the blank space below each column.

Prophet	Server	Teacher	Exhorter	Giver	Admin	Mercy
50 _2_	51 _0_	52 _3_	53 _1_	54 _0_	55 _1_	56 _0_
57 _2_	58 _0_	59 _3_	60 _3_	61 _1_	62 _1_	63 _1_
64 _2_	65 _1_	66 _3_	67 _3_	68 _0_	69 _2_	70 _1_
71 _3_	72 _1_	73 _3_	74 _2_	75 _1_	76 _1_	77 _0_
78 _3_	79 _2_	80 _3_	81 _1_	82 _0_	83 _1_	84 _0_
85 _3_	86 _0_	87 _3_	88 _2_	89 _0_	90 _1_	91 _1_
92 _3_	93 _1_	94 _3_	95 _3_	96 _1_	97 _3_	98 _1_
__18__	__5__	__21__	__15__	__3__	__10__	__4__
Auxiliary		**Primary**	**Tertiary**			
2nd	5th	**1st**	**3rd**	7th	4th	6th

From the scores above, we can see that this person's Motivational Gifts **PAT-Mix** is *Teacher / Prophet / Exhorter.*

Primary — Teacher = score 21
Auxiliary — Prophet = score 18
Tertiary — Exhorter = score 15
Mix

Appendix A

A Review of the Historical Development of the Motivational Gifts Theory

Special note to the Reader

The material in this appendix will likely be of interest to only a small portion of the readers of this text. Many will be interested in only the practical portions of this book which have to do with identifying and exercising their giftedness. Others may be interested in some of the theological, philosophical, and historical issues related to the Motivational-Gifts theory. For those of you who like the academic history of a topic, please continue reading.

Introduction to the Historical Development of the Motivational Gifts Theory

The available material on the gifts in Romans 12:6-8 being a set of personality types is scant at best. The reason is that there is no common agreement concerning these particular gifts, and not everyone agrees that these gifts represent personality types.

Not only are there the ever-present disagreements between Charismatics and those who are not, but there are also differences of perspectives and opinions within each group in respect to the validity of seeing the Romans 12:6-8 gifts as Motivational Gifts, and thus as personality types.

Furthermore, these differences must be inferred from the various writings since no academics (until now) have dealt head-on with the issue of *motivational-gifts theory*. Some authors (and lecturers) seem to promote the motivational-gifts theory while others expound on the

Romans 12 gifts from what might be considered "conventional wisdom."

Admittedly, those who believe that these gifts can be viewed as personality types have less exegetical ground from which to draw their conclusions. In fact, very few if any of those who seem to imply a *motivational gifts* idea do any exegetical work in support of this theory. Most generally, these people rely on the empirical data of evidence in people's lives. This means that they will often say that this idea of the gifts "seems to fit well" with what is known about personality types.

Yet, curiously, the label *theory* has not been used by those who see these gifts as personality types even though it seems that the burden of proof would be upon them. One cannot presume to know the basis of their teachings, but it seems apparent that those who promote the personality-types interpretation of the gifts see their perspective as accepted fact and in no need of defense.

Another curious aspect of these two fundamentally different ways of viewing these gifts is that neither seems to have addressed the other in any *extended manner*. Thus, one may read two very opposing views of the basic understanding and interpretation of the Romans 12:6-8 gifts without seeing an apologetic for either perspective. In other words, there does not seem to be an open debate. Each camp apparently is content to simply expound its own interpretation. A few statements have been given to the "debate," but few people have presented a defense of their position or a rebuttal of the opposing position. One wonders if some of the authors and lecturers who have promoted one or the other basic understanding of these gifts even realize the disparity between the two views or if each is even aware of the other's perspective.

It appears, however, that there are verbal apologetics, defenses, and rebuttals which arise from time to time during conversations. Some Classical Pentecostals whom I have interviewed see the idea of "personality-types theory" as a way to interpret and understand the gifts in Romans 12:6-8 as an anti-Pentecostal hermeneutical approach to the passage. In their estimation, the "personality-types theory" is a sliding into anti-supernaturalism because to them, it removes the supernatural aspects of these gifts. Furthermore, to some, the idea that psychology can play a part in understanding these gifts from the "personality-types theory" approach is simply a clear sign of "heresy."

Therefore, this *literature* review will attempt to cover what little has been said within the inferred "debate" and then simply point out which perspective is being represented. This review will be divided into three camps. From the theological perspective, two of these camps are represented: (1) Those who see the gifts from the conventional perspective, i.e., not personality types. (2) Those that see the gifts as personality types. And, camp three is a psychological perspective: (3) Those that offer some understanding of personality theory from a non-Christian psychological, and thus non-biblical, approach.

The Conventional Review

While many books have been written over the years on the topic of spiritual gifts, and some appear in the bibliography, I review a few representative texts here. It should be clearly understood that the perspectives of conventional and personality-types theory are not simply divided along theological camps. Some Pentecostals/ Charismatics are as opposed to the idea of personality-types theory (in relation to the gifts) as those outside Pentecostal/Charismatic persuasions; in fact, in some cases, more so. One of the well-known standard-bearers of the Classical Pentecostal perspective is Stanley M. Horton. His book, *What the Bible Says About the Holy Spirit*, has been a Pentecostal-sanctioned authority in conventional wisdom since it was first published over twenty years ago.[1] In the personality-types theory perspective, the gifts are not only seen individually but they are divided into categories. For example, the gifts delineated in 1 Corinthians 12 are seen as the *Manifestations of the Spirit*. The list in Ephesians 4:11 are referred to as the *Ministry Gifts*. And, Romans 12: 6-8 are the *Motivational* (i.e., personality types) *Gifts*. However, Horton unceremoniously states that Paul is not concerned with classifying or categorizing the gifts.[2] To buttress this idea, Horton goes on to combine the gifts from the various lists to arrive at a total of 18 to 20 gifts.[3]

Horton's *coup de grâce*—at least from his perspective— is found on page 262 of his book. Here, he states that the attempt to distinguish the "more supernatural" and "less supernatural" gifts by placing them in certain categories is simply wrong and non-exegetical.[4] However, Horton misunderstands the theory of the Motivational Gifts. This theory is not claiming that some gifts are supernatural and some are natural.

But, before one is too hard on Horton (and other

Classical Pentecostals), it should be understood that he is responding to the erroneous teachings of some that certain gifts *are* "more supernatural" and some are "less supernatural." One need not look far to find statements supporting the very thing that Horton decries. William McRae makes some irresponsible statements in this regard when he says that certain miraculous gifts ceased and then compares those who speak in tongues with Gnostics, Mormons, Moslems, and Eskimos![5] With indictments like this, one can understand the extreme responses of some Classical Pentecostals to the idea of "less supernatural" gifting. C. Peter Wagner indicates that there was quite a battle over this issue in 1918 when Benjamin B. Warfield was writing arguments against the miraculous gifts.[6]

However, it should be clearly understood that the "personality-types theory" (i.e., Motivational-Gifts theory) does not force the Bible to distinguish between gifts that are "more supernatural" and "less supernatural." While some authors may have contrived this erroneous distinction, I have attempted to clarify what the Motivational-Gifts theory is, and what each motivational gift is, and I did so on the basis that these motivational gifts *are* supernatural gifts because they have a supernatural source.

The Motivational-Gifts theory does not force the Bible to distinguish between gifts that are "more supernatural" and "less supernatural."

The manifestations of these gifts may be a simple

exercise of one's personhood, but the gifts themselves are supernatural to be sure. One should note also that Classical Pentecostals argue that even some of the more demonstrative gifts—such as speaking in tongues—are *under the exercise of one's will* as well. Concerning these more demonstrative gifts such as the gifts of healings and tongues, Horton says some people are wrong to think that these gifts are beyond the Christian's control. The classical passage of Scripture used in defense of the idea that the individual is, or at least should be, in control of the "manifestations of the Spirit" is 1 Corinthians 14:32, where Paul clearly says: "The spirits of prophets are subject to the control of prophets."

It has long been argued by clear-thinking Pentecostals that Christians should manifest the gifts of the Spirit with decorum befitting a move of the Holy Spirit for the purpose of spiritual edification. Therefore, if there should be such "control" of the manifestation of the more demonstrative gifts of the Spirit, should not this same latitude be extended to the less demonstrative gifts, e.g., administration, giving, mercy, *et al.*?

Therefore, the human exercise of these motivational gifts does not suggest that the "personality-types theory" must lead to an anti-supernaturalistic interpretation of Romans 12:6-8. When Horton says that *all* the gifts of the Spirit are part of the work of the Holy Spirit, his statement is echoed in the "personality-types theory" interpretation of Romans 12:6-8 as defined in this research.

Other Pentecostal writers from this era were so given to the "supernaturalness" of the gifts that sometimes their books did not even deal with the gifts found in Romans (nor

Ephesians). Harold Horton and Donald Gee are two such authors who, like Stanley Horton, represent the conventional wisdom. However, unlike Stanley Horton, both of their books deal exclusively with the gifts of the Spirit found in 1 Corinthians 12: Word of Wisdom, Word of Knowledge, Discerning of Spirits, Faith, Workings of Miracles, Gifts of Healings, Prophecy, Tongues, Interpretation of Tongues. Throughout his book, Donald Gee stresses the supernatural aspect of the gifts of the Spirit.

Early Pentecostal scholars and writers defended the supernaturalness of the gifts of the Spirit, and they seemed to conclude that the concept of motivational gifts, i.e., personality types, was an *affront* to the supernatural aspect of the gifts. Harold Horton is no exception. He too stresses the supernatural aspect of the gifts.

In brief, the conventional wisdom demonstrated in these three books was simply that all gifts are supernatural. However, conventional wisdom often takes a further step to conclude that since this is the case, the idea that gifts of the Spirit can be personality types leads to the idea that they are non-supernatural. Hence, for them, the Motivational Gifts theory is an incorrect way to view the gifts in Romans 12:6-8.

However, they misunderstand the Motivational Gifts theory. It attempts to view only a particular aspect of these gifts. That is, it views the personalities of the people who have the gifts. This is done without denying the conventional view. Thus, these two views work together to see not only the gifts but the people of the gifts.

The Gifts as Personality Types Review

Interestingly, in the Classical Pentecostal camp a shift toward the "personality-types theory" (i.e., Motivational-Gifts theory) may be emerging. Classical Pentecostal David Lim, an ordained Assemblies of God minister, seems to be recognizing the validity of the Motivational-Gifts theory and is helping to bridge the gap between the conventional perspective and the Motivational-Gifts theory. Lim makes several interesting points. He admits to the idea that some people have separated the gifts into the three major categories. While his terms are not the same that I used in this book, the basic distinction of these three groups is the same. He lists them as "motivational gifts" (Romans 12: 6-8), which is the same nomenclature that I have applied to them. The second category is listed as the "power gifts," (1 Corinthians 12: 8-10) which I refer to as the *Manifestations of the Spirit*. And, finally, he calls the third category the "leadership gifts" (Ephesians 4:11-13), which I call the *Ministry Gifts*.[7]

Even though Lim does not openly embrace these distinctions and categories, he does list them in a rather friendly way; and, while he is quick to point out the need for understanding function over category (and I agree with him on this point), he nonetheless appears to be sympathetic to the categories.

Perhaps, however, the biggest move toward the idea of the Motivational-Gifts theory is Lim's statement, which is out of character for a Classical Pentecostal scholar, that some gifts may appear more supernatural than the others but they are not.[8] This is exactly what the Motivational-Gifts theory teaches. The more demonstrative gifts of

1 Corinthians 12 are no more supernatural than the Motivational Gifts of Romans 12; they (the 1 Corinthians 12 gifts) just *appear* so. This seems to have been the hurdle that earlier Classical Pentecostals could not get over. They used the outwardly demonstrative supernatural aspect of the 1 Corinthians 12 gifts as the exemplar. If an interpretation of the Romans 12 gifts did not result in an outwardly supernatural manifestation (like the 1 Corinthians 12 gifts), they were inclined to reject it. However, Lim seems to turn the Classical-Pentecostal hermeneutics upside down and imply that the majority of the gifts do not appear supernatural, with the *exception* of the 1 Corinthians 12 gifts. However, even though they outwardly "appear" to be more supernatural than the other two sets of gifts (i.e., the Motivational Gifts of Romans 12: 6-8 and the Ministry Gifts of Ephesians 4: 11-14), they are not.

Thus, rather than making the Manifestations of the Spirit *the standard* and forcing the other gifts into their outwardly demonstrative mold, Lim seems to indicate that the gifts of the Spirit are relatively quiet in appearance and that the Manifestations of the Spirit (or "power gifts" as he calls them) are the *exception* to the rule. This basic shift in perspective will go a long way to helping people accept the other gifts of the Spirit under the categorization that this research is explicating.

Lim moves cautiously, however, and he correctly says that there is a lack of exegetical support for these categories. Also, he points out that the gifts overlap in functions, and so it is difficult to be dogmatic on this point. This is wise.

Since the Motivational-Gifts theory is a *theory* and not something explicitly stated in Scripture, it is important to sound this caveat. Nonetheless, some exegesis, sanctified reasoning, and empirical data seem to suggest that the Motivational-Gifts theory, while not explicitly taught in Scripture, is a legitimate way to view the Romans 12:6-8 gifts.

Lim seems to agree with this conclusion when he says that it might not be so much a question of biblical theology as much as a question of church dynamics. In other words, what is God doing in the lives of individual people with regard to these gifts?[9] If Lim is representative of emerging Classical Pentecostals—the fact that the Gospel Publishing House has published his book indicates that this may be the case—then there seems to be a shift in the *conventional wisdom* toward accepting the Motivational-Gifts theory. However, Lim does not expound the Motivational-Gifts theory point by point. He describes the gifts of the Spirit in a conventional-type way and at the same time opens the door to the acceptance of the Motivational-Gifts theory perspective.

David Allan Hubbard—not a Classical Pentecostal—in his text, *Unwrapping Your Spiritual Gifts*,[10] expounds on the Romans 12: 6-8 gifts in such a way that it would be considered very friendly towards the Motivational-Gifts theory. Again, it should be noted that one should *not expect* to find the Motivational-Gifts theory *per se* expounded. It is a theory that has received some attention, but by and large the academic community has chosen to simply expound on the gifts, not the theory. As pointed out above, there seems to be no desire to "debate" the validity of one's perspective on the gifts. Each writer, for the most part, is satisfied simply to present his perspective as though it were fact and leave it at that.

One aspect of Hubbard's text which is contra Motivational-Gifts theory is his statement that spiritual gifts are just *for Christians*. However, the Motivational-Gifts theory holds that all people have motivational gifts because they are, in fact, personality types, and all people are born with personality. This is not the same as the gifts of 1 Corinthians 12 and Ephesians 4, however. They belong only to those who are truly born-again and in whom the Holy Spirit dwells.

Non-Christians are a Part of God's Creation Too

Some people talk and write about non-Christians as though they created themselves! They speak of non-Christians as though they were not a part of God's creation. But, they are. The issue then is not, "Does God give spiritual gifts to non-Christians?" Rather, the issue is that when people become saved, they should exercise their already-God-given *motivations* for the glory of God, through the power of the Holy Spirit, and for the edification of the Body of Christ.

Thus, the Motivational-Gifts theory states that all people are born with their motivational gifts, and when they are "born-again" (i.e., become Christians), they can then begin to use those motivations in a Christian context to fulfill God's will for their lives. Again, exegesis may not yield this understanding, but as David Lim has stated, the issue may be more about what God is uniquely doing in individual lives rather than one of biblical theology.[11] This is not to say that one can go outside the intent of Scripture, but when a theory or understanding is in keeping with the tenor of Scripture and does not do injustice to the truths therein, then one may safely arrive at truth which is in keeping with God's purposes. The idea of inherent motivational giftedness, i.e., God-given personality types, seems to be in accord with the Creator aspect of God found in Scripture. In fact, given that the Scriptures indicate that God is at work in the forming of children in the womb, one would be hard-pressed to argue that God does not play an active part in each person's personality formation. The Psalmist states:

For you created my inmost being; you knit me together in my mother's womb. I praise you because I am fearfully and wonderfully made; your works are wonderful, I know that full well. My frame was not hidden from you when I was made in the secret place. When I was woven together in the depths of the earth, your eyes saw my unformed body. All the days ordained for me were written in your book before one of them came to be (Ps. 139:13-16).

Moving even closer to the Motivational-Gifts theory is C. Peter Wagner.[12] In his book *Your Spiritual Gifts Can Help Your Church Grow*, he lays the groundwork for more specific aspects of Motivational-Gifts theory. It may have been Wagner who, in these recent times, introduced the concept of "gift-mixes" (or PAT-Mix as I call them, more about this later). This is a salient point in Motivational-

Gifts theory which states that each person may (and most generally do) have more than one gift. The combination of the gifts that a person has is called his gift-mix. Also, Wagner moves from simply stating what a gift is to what the person who has that gift is like. In this is seen a movement in the direction of the Motivational-Gifts theory. To the extent that he moves from describing the gift to describing the person who has the gift, he is moving toward, or laying the basis for, the Motivational-Gifts theory. However, Wagner does not stop with just the seven gifts of Romans 12: 6-8. He describes twenty-seven gifts including the Manifestations of the Spirit found in 1 Corinthians 12.

This confusing of the categories between Motivational Gifts and Manifestations of the Spirit shows that while Wagner was moving toward the Motivational-Gifts theory, he did not make the category distinctions that are necessary for the Motivational-Gifts theory. In the Motivational-Gifts theory, the person of the gift is described. For example, a Motivational Gift of Prophet is a person who has a worldview which is very "black and white." Things for this person are divided into right and wrong. This description of the person of the gift rather than the gift itself cannot be done when the *Manifestations of the Spirit* are the topic. For example, one cannot simply identify a tongues-gifted individual from the perspective of personality characteristics. However, the mixing of categories notwithstanding, Wagner has made a significant contribution to the development of the Motivational-Gifts theory.

Very close to the type of work that Wagner did is the

work of Charles V. Bryant in *Rediscovering the Charismata*.[13] However, like Wagner, Bryant mixes the categories, which is evident from his need to describe the person of the gift in some cases, and then describe the gift itself in other cases. Still, it appears that this lesser-known book helped move some thinkers towards the Motivational-Gifts theory.

The jump to the Motivational-Gifts theory without mixing the categories *may* have come first from Bill Gothard.[14] While he did not publish a book *per se* on this topic, he did make available some print-outs which explored this aspect of giftedness. Gothard's research deals exclusively with the Motivational Gifts found in Romans 12. It shows that different people representing different Motivational Gifts will respond to the same situation in different ways. While Gothard's work sees the Romans 12 gifts from the Motivational-Gifts theory, it lacks sophistication. However, what it lacks in sophistication, it may make up in its benefit of having been used in practical applications for hundreds if not thousands of people, and from that empirical data, Gothard was able to conclude that the Motivational-Gifts theory seemed to be confirmed in the practical lives of those who participated in his teachings on this topic.

The next step in the Motivational-Gifts theory was to clearly categorize the gifts of the Spirit into the three categories mentioned above. This was done—but not without some exegetical problems—by a husband and wife team, Don and Katie Fortune.[15] In their book, *Discover Your God-Given Gifts*, they expound on the Romans 12 gifts from the same perspective that this present research takes, i.e., personality types. However, the Fortunes' work lacks sophistication, proper biblical exegesis, and academic scholarship. Also, their argumentation is often over-stated. For example, one curious aspect of their exposition of the Motivational Gifts is their arbitrary renaming of the gift of prophecy to "perceiver." They claim to be making this name change for the sake of clarification, but they ultimately lead the reader away from the biblically correct term and thus away from accurately understanding this biblical gift. They discuss the gifts from a practical perspective using the *application* of this theory *in the church as their guide to validity*. By the time they published their book, the Fortunes had taught motivational gifts seminars for 12 years.[16] They testify that the practical application of the motivational gifts validates the Motivational-Gifts theory (although they do not refer to it as a *theory* as I am doing).

The Psychological Perspective Review

While there are various books that deal with the subject of personality theory, there are a couple that seem to "cross-over" and include the idea that the personality types are gifts from God.

While not making the bridge *between* personality theory and motivational gifts, Harbaugh nonetheless identifies the fact that some God-given gifts are our own personhood or personality. Harbaugh is professor of pastoral care and psychology at a Lutheran seminary. Throughout his book, he stresses the idea that God has gifted each of us; this supports his foundational teaching on personality theory. Harbaugh does not make the connection that I am attempting to explore, but he rather expounds on psychological theory, specifically that found in Carl Jung and Isabel Briggs Myers. One might say that while my book is biblically oriented, expounding on the gifts that God has given us and I use the psychological types theory for reinforcement, Harbaugh turns the tables, and his book is psychologically oriented, expounding on psychological types that Carl Jung has identified, and he uses the Bible for reinforcement.

Next, a very interesting book with a most captivating title is *Gifts Differing* by Isabel Briggs Myers and Peter Myers.[17] What makes this book interesting is that it may be the single best text to introduce people to the research and understanding of psychological type theory as founded by Carl Jung and expounded by Isabel Briggs Myers. The authors describe the insights that are found in the Myers-Briggs Type Indicator (MBTI). The MBTI identifies 16 personality types, and this book clearly explains what each of these types is. It is an essential piece of research for the understanding of the MBTI personality theory. The title of their book, *Gifts Differing* is, interestingly, taken from Romans 12:6, "Having then, gifts differing, according to the grace that is given to us (KJV)."

Now, unlike Harbaugh's text using Scripture as support for the concept of psychological types, *Gifts Differing* uses Scripture only for its title and for its concluding remarks as it closes with an edited version of Romans 12:4-8. However, I think that it is fitting to conclude this chapter with the unedited version:

Just as each of us has one body with many
members, and these members do not all have the
same function, so in Christ we who are many form
one body, and each member belongs to all the others.
We have different gifts, according to the grace given
us. If a man's gift is prophesying, let him use it in
proportion to his faith. If it is serving, let him serve; if
it is teaching, let him teach; if it is encouraging, let
him encourage; if it is contributing to the needs of
others, let him give generously; if it is leadership, let
him govern diligently; if it is showing mercy, let him
do it cheerfully (Romans 12:4-8).

---

[1] S. M. Horton, *What the Bible Says About the Holy Spirit* (Springfield, Mo.: Gospel Publishing House, 1976). On the dust-jacket of the 1986 printing of this text, it states that this book is the "result of a lifetime of dedicated study by one of the most respected Pentecostal scholars of our day, and will become a standard text in its field." Indeed it has.

[2] Ibid., p. 209.

[3] Ibid., p. 210.

[4] Ibid., p. 262.

[5] William J. McRae, *The Dynamics of Spiritual Gifts* (Grand Rapids, Mi.: Zondervan Publishing Co., 1976), p. 97.

[6] C. Peter Wagner, *Your Spiritual Gifts Can Help Your Church Grow* (Ventura, Ca.: Regal Books, 1979), p. 23.

[7] David Lim, *Spiritual Gifts: A Fresh Look* (Springfield, Mo.: Gospel Publishing House, 1991), p. 206.

[8] Ibid.

[9] Ibid.

[10] David Allan Hubbard, *Unwrapping Your Spiritual Gifts* (Waco, Tx.: Word Books Publisher, 1985). Hubbard was the president of Fuller Theological Seminary at the time of his writing this text.

[11] Lim, *Spiritual Gifts*, p. 206.

[12] C. Peter Wagner, *Your Spiritual Gifts Can Help your Church Grow* (Ventura, Ca.: Regal Books, 1979). On page 15 Wagner says, "As far as spiritual gifts are concerned, I do not identify with either the Pentecostal or Neo-Pentecostal or the Charismatic movements."

[13] Charles V. Bryant, *Rediscovering the Charismata* (Waco, Tx.: Word Books Publishers, 1986).

[14] Bill Gothard, *How to Understand Spiritual Gifts* (Oak Brook, Il.: Institute in Basic Life Principles, 1981).

[15] Don and Katie Fortune, *Discover Your God-Given Gifts* (Old Tappan, N.J.: Fleming H. Revell Company, 1987).

[16] Ibid., p. 9.

[17] Isabel Briggs Myers with Peter B. Myers, *Gifts Differing* (Palo Alto, Ca.: Consulting Psychologists Press Inc., 1980).

Appendix B

A Brief Theology of Spiritual Gifts

There are three major lists of gifts. These three main categories of spiritual gifts are:

1. Ministry Gifts (Ephesians 4)
2. Manifestations of the Spirit
   (1 Corinthians 12)
3. Motivational Gifts (Romans 12)

Below, I have listed the gifts in each category.

Category One
The Ministry Gifts

The Ministry Gifts of Ephesians 4

It was he who gave some to be apostles, some to be prophets, some to be evangelists, and some to be pastors (shepherds) and teachers, to prepare God's people for works of service, so that the body of Christ may be built up until we all reach unity in the faith and in the knowledge of the Son of God and become mature, attaining to the whole measure of the fullness of Christ (Ephesians 4:11-13).[1]

An important thing to understand about the gifts

listed in the Ephesians 4 passage is that they are not gifts in the same *sense* as those listed in 1 Corinthians 12. Notice that the Ephesians 4 list is actually a list of *people*, whereas the 1 Corinthians 12 list is a list of abstract gifts, not people.

The first gift in Ephesians 4 is the gift of apostle, *not apostleship*. Next is the gift of prophet, *not prophecy*. Next, it lists evangelist, *not evangelism*. Then, it also lists pastors and teachers, *not pastoring and teaching*. Thus, the Ephesians list is not talking about *charismata* (i.e., gifts) so much as it is talking about the *pneumatics*[2] (people) whom God has placed in the church.

> *The first gift in Ephesians 4 is the gift of apostle, not apostleship.*

We have all heard the sarcastic phrase that goes something like this: *"He thinks he is God's gift to women."* Well, these people in Ephesians 4 *are God's gifts* to the church. So, apostles are God's gifts to the church. Prophets are God's gifts to the church. Evangelists are God's gifts to the church. Pastors and teachers are God's gifts to the church.

The Term "Office"

Something that adds confusion to the issue of the gifts in Ephesians 4:11 is the term *office*. The term *office* is often loosely applied to the functions of these gifts. However, the Ephesians 4:11 gifts are not listed as the offices of the church, but rather as gifted individuals whom Christ has given to the church and who are responsible for equipping the saints for the work of ministry.

Thus, Ephesians 4:11 is not emphasizing *office designations*. Rather, the emphasis of Ephesians 4:11 are *gifted individuals*. Thus, the term *office* is not an appropriate label for the five gifts listed in Ephesians 4:11. Gordon Fee agrees and says that Paul's rhetoric in 1 Corinthians 12:28 implies that the apostles, prophets, and teachers are to be thought of as ministries and not as offices.[3] This is precisely the point: these gifted individuals are functioning *in ministries,* not offices, and some gifted teacher, for example, might teach a Sunday School class yet never fill the formal designation of an "office" in the church.

Neither an "office" nor an "intangible gift" can teach and prepare others for the work of the ministry. Only *people* have that ability. Yet, *these gifted individuals* are to "prepare [equip or train] God's people for works of service" (Eph. 4:12). Thus, this passage concentrates on the *person with the gift* rather than on some abstract gift or some supposed office.

Offices in the Church Bishop and Deacon

So, what offices *are* in the church? It appears from Scripture that there are two primary offices: that of Bishop and that of Deacon.

The Bishop

Bishop (*episkopos*) literally means an Overseer. Also, another biblical word denotes the same person: Elder (*presbyteros*). These three terms, *bishop, overseer,* and *elder* are not three different offices. There is one office with a person in that office fulfilling the function of these three terms: as a *bishop,* this individual *oversees* the church; and as an elder, this individual denotes spiritual maturity and understanding.[4] Notice how the book of Acts identifies the elders as overseers:

From Miletus, Paul sent to Ephesus for the **elders** of the church. When they arrived, he said **to them** . . . Keep watch over yourselves and all the flock of which the Holy Spirit has made you **overseers**. Be **shepherds** of the church of God, which he bought with his own blood (Acts 20:17-18; 28, emphasis added).

Paul says that these people are elders with the ministry of overseeing and shepherding the church. Note also Paul's reference to the bishop:

Here is a trustworthy saying: If anyone sets his heart on being an **overseer** [*bishop*], he desires a noble task. Now the **overseer** [*bishop*] must be above reproach, the husband of but one wife, temperate, self-controlled, respectable, hospitable, able to teach, not given to drunkenness, not violent but gentle, not quarrelsome, not a lover of money. He must manage his own family well and see that his children obey him with proper respect. (If anyone does not know how to manage his own family, how can he take care of God's church?) He must not be a recent convert, or he may become conceited and fall under the same judgment as the devil. He must also have a good reputation with outsiders, so that he will not fall into disgrace and into the devil's trap (1 Timothy 3:1-7, Emphasis added).

The Deacon

A deacon is an official in a local church. Paul speaks of this office:

Deacons, likewise, are to be men worthy of respect, sincere, not indulging in much wine, and not pursuing dishonest gain. They must keep hold of the deep truths of the faith with a clear conscience. They must first be tested; and then if there is nothing against them, let them serve as deacons. In the same way, their wives are to be women worthy of respect, not malicious talkers but temperate and trustworthy in everything. A deacon must be the husband of but one wife and must manage his children and his household well (1 Timothy 3:8-12).

The main emphasis of the word deacon is "server." This is clearly seen in the book of Acts where the early church selected its first deacons at the direction of Jesus' Twelve disciples:

In those days when the number of disciples was increasing, the Grecian Jews among them complained against the Hebraic Jews because their widows were being overlooked in the daily distribution of food. So the Twelve gathered all the disciples together and said, "It would not be right for us to neglect the ministry of the word of God in order to wait on tables. Brothers, choose seven men from among you who are known to be full of the Spirit and wisdom. We will turn this responsibility over to them and will give our attention to prayer and the ministry of the word." This proposal pleased the whole group. They chose Stephen, a man full of faith and of the Holy Spirit; also Philip, Procorus, Nicanor, Timon, Parmenas, and Nicolas from Antioch, a convert to Judaism. They presented these men to the apostles, who prayed and laid their hands on them (Acts 6:1-6).

Notice the responsibility of the deacons: they were *to serve others*. In fact, it appears that these seven deacons were the first "waiters." The issue which brought about their appointment was the distribution of food. In Acts 6:2 the disciples said, "It would not be right for us to neglect the ministry of the word of God in order to wait on tables." Thus, the deacons were to do these physically related duties of ministry.

This is not always how deacons are "used" in the modern church. I have seen some churches in which deacons are actually the leadership of the church in all its aspects. But, nonetheless, the Bible sees the position of deacon as an *office* which is related to the physical needs of service.

Only Two Offices in the Church

In brief, then, there are two offices in the church: **(1) the bishop** (also called *overseer* and *elder*), and **(2) deacon**. How these two offices play out in our modern churches vary, but the Bible seems to be clear that these are the two offices.

Two Sub-categories Within the Ministry Gifts

Let us now look more closely at these *person-gifts*. There are two sub-categories under the Ministry Gifts. There are the foundational gifts and the super-structural gifts. As in the building of any house, one must build the foundation and then the superstructure. The person-gifts of Ephesians 4:11 were to function as builders, each with its specific function.

A. Foundational (but not exclusively)
1. Apostles
2. Prophets

B. Super-structural
3. Evangelists
4. Pastors (shepherds)
5. Teachers

Category Two
Manifestations of the Spirit

Manifestations of the Spirit of 1 Corinthians 12

The next category of gifts is what is known as the *Manifestations of the Spirit*. The reason this title is given to this list of gifts is because it is not talking about people, but gifts which when exercised through Christians show forth the presence (or manifestation) of the Holy Spirit. For example, when a true gift of healing functions, one can be certain that the Holy Spirit has just manifested His presence.

Three Sub-categories Within the Manifestations

There are three sub-categories within the Manifestations of the Spirit: (a) *revelation gifts* by which God reveals something to a Christian; (b) *power gifts* by which God acting through human agency does something miraculous; and (c) *vocal gifts* by which God speaks to His people through an individual.

A. Revelation Gifts
1. Word of Wisdom
2. Word of Knowledge
3. Discerning of Spirits

B. Power Gifts

4. Faith
5. Workings of Miracles
6. Gifts of Healings

C. Vocal Gifts

7. Prophecy
8. Tongues
9. Interpretation of Tongues

Category Three
Motivational Gifts

Motivational Gifts of Romans 12

Finally, category three is that list of gifts that this book has reviewed and investigated. Like Ephesians 4 this is a list of people and not intangible gifts. However, unlike Ephesians 4, which is a list of people *and their ministry* in the church, Romans 12 is a list of people *and their personality types.*

1. Prophet
2. Server (helps—1 Corinthians 12:28)
3. Teacher
4. Exhorter
5. Giver
6. Administrator (governments—1 Corinthians 12:28)
7. Mercy

Now that we have *listed* the three main categories, we must now explain or describe them so it is clear what each gift is.

Gifts in Each Category Described

Category One
The Ministry Gifts of Ephesians 4

1. **Apostles** (means literally "sent ones" and connotes "a special messenger"[5]): These are those who both *saw* Jesus and *were commissioned* by Him. They were *sent by Him* as *His messengers.*

What They Are Not

There are two popular misunderstandings about the gift of apostle. One says that a person who starts churches is an apostle. The fact is that thousands (millions?) of Christians over the years have started churches, and they were not apostles. Church starting or church planting does not make you an apostle any more than planting a tree in your back yard makes you a *forest ranger.* I started/ planted a couple churches in my years as a pastor, but I am *not an apostle.* Some attempt to argue that since the Apostle Paul planted churches, anyone who plants churches must be an apostle. However, this fails to take two fundamental things into account: (1) Paul did many other things besides plant churches, and (2) some other disciples were called apostles and the Bible does not say that they planted churches.

The other popular misunderstanding is that an apostle is a Christian leader who oversees several churches or an entire district (sort of a "district manager"). However, this too is simply a false idea. Again, some argue that since Paul was over several churches and since he was an apostle, then others who are over several churches must likewise be apostles. The bad logic here is almost funny when applied to other things. For example, since Microsoft mogul Bill Gates is a billionaire, and since he has money, then others who have money must be billionaires. This is, of course, absurd.

What They Are

Here is the *key point* of describing (or defining) an apostle: It is not about *what they do*, but about *who commissioned them*, and *how they were commissioned*. Therefore, an apostle is one who has seen Jesus Christ (the who), face to face (the how), and received a *direct (personal, face to face)* calling from Him to preach the gospel. It is not within the scope of this book to deal with the validity of visions and appearances of Christ today,[6] but to be an apostle today, one would have to see Jesus in some visionary way and be commissioned by Him during that vision.

Also, it should be *pointed out* and *remembered* that only the early apostles were called to lay the church's foundation. The foundation has been laid, and no one can lay it again. In other words, there are no apostles today with the same calling or inspiration as the apostles of Christ in the New Testament. *Only* the *New Testament apostles* were *foundational-apostles*:

> Consequently, you are no longer foreigners and aliens, but fellow citizens with God's people and members of God's household, built on **the foundation of the apostles and prophets**, with Christ Jesus himself as the chief cornerstone (emphasis added, Eph. 2:19-20).

Therefore, for one to be an apostle today, one (1) must *have seen Jesus* in a visionary way (remember, this is how the apostle Paul saw Jesus when he was commissioned by Him—Acts 9:4ff.), (2) must be *commissioned by Christ* during that visionary experience, and (3) cannot be a foundational apostle, for the foundation of the household of God has already been laid and need not be laid again. Thus, an apostle today *does not* have the authority, inspiration, nor calling that the New Testament, foundational apostles had.

2. Prophets (a proclaimer of a divine message, under divine inspiration): Their words (i.e., God's Words spoken by them) edify, exhort, and comfort the hearers: "But everyone who prophesies speaks to men for their strengthening, encouragement and comfort" (1 Corinthians 14:3).

Like the apostles, there are no *foundational prophets* today. Also, like today's apostles, today's prophets do not have the same authority or inspiration as biblical prophets of old. Therefore, their words are *not* on par with, nor equal to, Scripture. In fact, the New Testament clearly tells us that, "All Scripture is God-breathed and is useful for teaching, rebuking, correcting and training in righteousness, so that the man of God may be thoroughly equipped for every good work" (2 Timothy 3:16-17). However, *prophecy* is given only for *strengthening*, *encouragement*, and *comfort*. "But everyone who prophesies speaks to men for their strengthening, encouragement and comfort" (1 Corinthians 14:3). Note again these different functions:

Scripture
   a. is *God-breathed*
   b. and is useful for *teaching*
   c. rebuking
   d. correcting
   e. training in righteousness

Prophecy
   a. is given to strengthen
   b. encourage
   c. comfort

Clearly then, prophecies are not on par with Scripture. Furthermore, the Apostle Paul teaches that prophecies must be judged (weighed carefully): "Two or three prophets should speak, and the others should weigh carefully what is said" (1 Corinthians 14:29). The mere fact that Paul says prophecies must be weighed carefully implies that the non-foundational, New Testament prophets are fallible. Also, since all prophecies must be judged, it would be wise for those who prophesy to refrain from the stern "Thus says the Lord."

3. Evangelists (bringers of good news): Preachers to the lost.

4. Pastors (shepherds): Feeders and protectors. This title is often misunderstood. While the word pastor in this passage may apply to a person who is in the position of a pastor in a local church, this word is not depicting someone who manages or works as the leader of a local church. This word "pastor" is better translated as "shepherd." People can be "shepherds" within a local church without being the "Senior Pastor" of that church. This shepherding means to "feed the flock of God" and to "guide the flock of God." Thus, in early church times, this gift of "pastor/shepherd" was often seen in those who were bishops (overseers, elders).

5. Teachers (instructors): Those who help equip the saints by teaching them God's truths.

Category Two
Manifestations of the Spirit
of 1 Corinthians 12

A. Revelation Gifts

1. Word of Wisdom: The word of wisdom is *logos sophias* (literally: message or utterance of wisdom). A word of wisdom, then, is an utterance of a fragment of God's infinite wisdom imparted to a believer by the Holy Spirit for the purpose of solving a problem, answering a question, or clearly expressing the will of God.

An example of this in the life of Jesus Christ may be seen when some were trying to trick him with regard to paying taxes. Jesus asked them whose inscription was on the coin. Then, he gave a word of wisdom which did all three: solved a problem, answered a question, and clearly expressed the will of God:

> "Show me the coin used for paying the tax." They brought him a denarius, and he asked them, "Whose portrait is this? And whose inscription?" "Caesar's," they replied. Then he said to them, "Give to Caesar what is Caesar's, and to God what is God's." *When they heard this, they were amazed.* So they left him and went away (emphasis added, Matthew 22:19-21).

2. Word of Knowledge: The word of knowledge is

logos gnosis (literally: message or utterance of knowledge). Thus, it is a fragment of God's knowledge imparted to a believer by the Holy Spirit. Through this gift, the Holy Spirit makes known to a person something that God knows but that the receiver does not. There could be a number of reasons why God would impart a fragment of His knowledge to someone. He might impart a specific understanding of Scripture to someone. He might impart a fragment of His knowledge to someone of an impending disaster of a loved one so that the person might pray for the person in trouble. He might impart a fragment of His divine knowledge to a Christian counselor about a person whom he or she is helping.

An example of this gift in operation in the life of Peter may be seen in Acts chapter five where the word of knowledge is given to reveal corruption in the hearts of the married couple Ananias and Sapphira. Peter received "inside" information about the deceit of Ananias and Sapphira. They were attempting to lie to the apostles concerning a certain real estate transaction. However, Peter received a *word of knowledge* from the Holy Spirit revealing the deceptive nature of the couple's actions. When Ananias lied to Peter, God revealed to Peter the deception through this *word of knowledge*, and Peter said, "Ananias, how is it that Satan has so filled your heart that you have lied to the Holy Spirit and have kept for yourself some of the money you received for the land" (Acts 5:3)? Peter knew something at that moment that he had no way of knowing unless God had imparted it to him by divine revelation.

3. Discerning of Spirits: Discerning of Spirits is *diakrisis pneumaton* (literally: distinguishing of spirits). This is the divinely imparted ability to know (discern) the presence of God's Spirit, evil spirits, or human spirits. People often perpetuate confusion and error by speaking of the *"gift of discernment"* as if there were such a gift in 1 Corinthians 12:10. There is not. Note well, the *"gift of discernment"* is fallacious and non-existent. The correct title, and correct gift is the "gift of Discerning of Spirits." Note the significant difference in the two appellations.

Since this is the *gift of discerning of spirits* and not the so-called *gift of discernment*, it is not the ability to know something personal about another person. Some people who claim to have this dubious "gift of discernment" (or personal insight into the lives and minds of others) are often simply adept at being critical of others. These people *claim* to have "God's inside information" about others.

I once met a women (a so-called "prophetess") who claimed to have this fallacious gift. She would sit in a restaurant and point out people throughout the room and start saying what was going on in their lives and what was wrong with their personalities or characteristics, and what sins they were in. Rather than challenging her exegetically, I asked her to accompany me to actually talk to those people she claimed to have insights on, but she refused. How could she possibly know that these things were going on in the lives of these people if she didn't confirm her "revelations" by talking with the people themselves?

Notice that when Peter received a revelation about Ananias, he spoke to him about it (Acts 5)! It was abundantly evident that this women was a fraud. Not only did she claim a gift that simply did not exist, but she never confirmed her "revelations" and simply expected people to believe whatever she "perceived" about others. (By the way, she "perceived" that I was unspiritual and obstinate because I would not accept her "giftedness from God.")

Discerning of spirits is for the distinguishing of *spirits*, not personalities or flawed characteristics in people. An actual case of discernings of spirits comes to us from the book of Acts. Acts 16 records that a slave girl possessed by an evil spirit followed Paul and his companions and shouted out, "These men are servants of the most high God, who are telling you the way to be saved" (Acts 16:17). Though her words may seem good to some, her actions flowed from the wrong spirit. Finally, after a few days, Paul commanded the evil spirit to come out of her. It appears, then, that Paul knew of her evil spirit possession by divine revelation, a discernings of spirits. Remember, this is the *gift of discernings of spirits*, not the "gift of discernment."

Discerning of spirits is for the distinguishing of spirits, not personalities or flawed characteristics in people.

B. Power Gifts

4. Faith: The word faith is *pistis* (literally: a firm persuasion). It should be remembered that this is the *gift of faith*; thus, it is not the same thing as "regular faith." This particular *faith* is the divine impartation of a total trust in God which produces a calm control in the face of extreme difficulties. This is the *God-given active condition of the spirit of a person holding on to the truth and trusting in the fact that God can do anything.* It is the supernatural ability that God imparts to some Christians when it is needed to believe Him for the unbelievable; it is the supernatural capacity to turn one's life over to God in the most difficult situations.

A biblical example of this particular kind of faith (*gift of faith*) is seen in the life of the prophet Daniel. He was thrown into a den of lions (Daniel 6:16-23). During his "sleep-over" with the lions, he did not rebuke the lions, nor did he command them not to eat him. Daniel's faith showed no such outward action as rebuking or commanding. However, there was action in his spirit. The Scripture records, "And when Daniel was lifted from the den, no wound was found on him, because he *had trusted* in his God" (emphasis added, 6:23b).

This exercise of the gift of faith in this instance may be referred to as "calm control." For that is exactly how Daniel handled the problem: he was calm, and through the faith that God gave him, he was in control (i.e., he remained composed).

5. Workings of Miracles: The Greek words are *energema dunamis* (literally *energy power*). The workings of miracles is God *and man* acting together to produce the supernatural. The Bible is full of such miracles. Two outstanding accounts are seen in the life of Moses: (1) the parting of the Red Sea as Moses lifted his rod, and (2) water from the rock as Moses struck the rock with his rod.

It needs to be understood that the gift called a *workings of miracles* is not the same thing as miracles. A miracle is simply God's sovereign operation of producing a miracle. In the *gift of the workings of miracles,* God is the agent Who gives the power and the person is the instrument whom God uses to bring about the miraculous. To help clarify the distinction between miracles and the *working of miracles*, a table is given below showing some biblical examples of the two categories:

Miracles Table

Workings of Miracles God Working with Humans	Sovereign Miracles God Working Alone
Part Red Sea, Ex. 14:13-16, 21-22	Creation, Gen. 1:1
Water from the Rock, Ex. 17:6	Confusion of tongues, Gen. 11:7-9
Sun stands still, Josh 10:12	Manna from heaven, Ex. 16:4
Axhead floats, 2 Kings 6:5-7	Donkey talks, Num. 22:27-31
Calms wind and waves, Matt. 8:26	Shoes don't wear out, Deut. 29:5
Water to wine, John 2	Resurrection of Christ, Mark 16
Raising Dorcas, Acts 9:40	Catching away Philip, Acts 8:39
Blinding of Elymas, Acts 13:11	Blinding of Saul, Acts 9:3-9

Obviously, God does not need a human's assistance to produce a miracle. However, the gift of the *workings of miracles* is brought about with a person's active involvement: *the workings of miracles is a co-operative act between God and His chosen human vessel.*

6. Gifts of Healings: This phrase in Greek is *charismata iamaton* (literally *gifts of healings*, both plural). This gift is the God-given ability to heal people afflicted with various sicknesses and diseases. The gifts of healings is not to be confused with sovereign healings. God may and does heal without any human instrumentality. The *gifts of healings*, however, is a partnership act between God and a human through whom the Holy Spirit manifests himself by healing a person in need. However, the person so used does *not* become a "healer." God alone is the healer, and people are healed when He touches them through His human instrumentality.

C. Vocal Gifts

7. Prophecy: In 1 Corinthians 12:10, the gift of prophecy is *propheteia* (literally: to speak forth). Prophecy, then, is a supernatural speaking of God's Word, in the common language, for the purpose of edification, exhortation, and comfort. This is not preaching. Some have attempted to identify the gift of prophecy with preaching, but such an understanding is not supported by Scripture.

8. Tongues: The Greek word for tongue is *glossa*, and the Greek word for speak is *lalia*. Thus, *glossolalia* is to speak in tongues. The gift of speaking in tongues is a supernatural speaking in another language for the purpose of edification, exhortation, and comfort, or speaking to God in prayer and/or worship.

9. Interpretation of Tongues: The gift of interpretation (*hermaneia*: literally, interpretation) of tongues is the God-given ability to understand the meaning of a message in tongues and to speak forth that interpretation so that others may understand the message and be edified.

Category Three
Motivational Gifts (Romans 12)

Since it is this list with which this book has been concerned and has expounded, I will give only a very brief description here.

1. Prophet: Truth speaker. One who speaks the truth as one perceives it to be without fear of others.

2. Server: (also, helps in 1 Corinthians 12:28) One who helps others by meeting their practical, physical needs.

3. Teacher: One who thinks from logical and analytical perspectives, and communicates from that rationale.

4. Exhorter: One who is an encourager.

5. Giver: One who shares one's financial and material wealth with people or ministries in need.

6. Administrator: (also, governments in 1 Corinthians 12:28)

One who thinks from a managerial perspective and who likes to coordinate and direct activities to reach a common goal.

7. Mercy: One who identifies with and shares in the sorrow of others for the purpose of comforting them.

---

1 It should be noted that the noun "pastors" in this passage does not mean the same thing as is commonly thought of today. The idea of a "pastor" today is someone who is the primary preacher and chief administrator of a local church. This was not the meaning in this passage. In fact, the Greek word for "pastor" may be better translated as shepherd, and means one who cares for the flock. And, while a pastor in the modern-day sense may be doing that, many people in the church can be shepherds without being the pastor of the church.

2 The term *pneumatics* is used here to denote *gifted people*. In this context, I am simply attempting to make the distinction between the gifts (*charismata)* and the people (*pneumatics*) who function in the gifts.

3 F. F. Bruce, gen. ed., *The New International Commentary on the New Testament* (Grand Rapids: Eerdmans Publishing Co., 1987): *The First Epistle to the Corinthians*, by Gordon Fee, p. 619.

4 W. E. Vine, Merrill F. Unger, and William White, Jr., *An Expository Dictionary of Biblical Words* (Nashville, Tn.: Thomas Nelson Publishers, 1984), p. 67.

5 D. A. Carson argues that the term *apostle* in the New Testament suggests that rather than "sent one" the meaning is "a special representative" or "a special messenger." While the difference may appear minor, it is nonetheless noteworthy in conjunction with his discussion of the "root fallacy": *Exegetical Fallacies* (Grand Rapids: Baker Book House, 1984). pp. 26-29.

6 Visionary experiences with the risen Christ happened to those who

were *not foundational prophets* even in New Testament times: "In Damascus there was a disciple named Ananias. The Lord called to him in a vision, 'Ananias!' 'Yes, Lord,' he answered" (Acts 9:10).

Selected Bibliography

Barclay, William. The Promise of the Spirit. Philadelphia, Pa: The Westminster Press, 1976.

Bennett, Dennis, and Rita. The Holy Spirit and You. Plainfield, N.J.: Logos International, 1971.

Bittlinger, Arnold. Gifts and Graces. Grand Rapids, Mi.: Wm. B. Eerdmans Publishing Co., 1967.

_____ . Gifts and Ministries. Grand Rapids, Mi.: Wm. B. Eerdmans Publishing Co., 1973.

Bridge, Donald and Phypers, David. Spiritual Gifts and the Church. Downers Grove, Il.: Inter-Varsity Press, 1973.

Brumback, Carl. What Meaneth This? Springfield, Mo.: Gospel Publishing House, 1947.

Bryant, Charles V. Rediscovering the Charismata. Waco, Tx.: Word Books Publishers, 1986.

Carlson, G. Raymond. Spiritual Dynamics. Springfield, Mo.: Gospel Publishing House, 1976.

Carson, D. A. From Triumphalism to Maturity. Grand Rapids, Mi.: Baker Book House, 1984.

_____. Showing the Spirit. Grand Rapids, Mi.: Baker Book House, 1987.

Clinton, Bobby. Spiritual Gifts. Beaverlodge, Alberta, Canada: Horizon House Publishers, 1985.

Cook, Jerry. Love, Acceptance and Forgiveness. Glendale, Ca.: Regal Books, 1980.

Criswell, W. A. The Baptism, Filling, & Gifts of the Holy Spirit. Grand Rapids, Mi.: Zondervan Publishing House, 1973.

Ervin, Howard M. These are not Drunken as Ye Suppose. Plainfield, N.J.: Logos International, 1968.

Flyn, Leslie B. Nineteen Gifts of the Spirit. Wheaton, Il.: Victor Books, 1974.

Fortune, Don and Katie. Discover Your God-Given Gifts. Old Tappan, N.J.: Fleming H. Revell Company, 1987.

_____. Discover Your Children's Gifts. Old Tappan, N.J.: Fleming H. Revell Company, 1989.

Gangel, Kenneth O. You and Your Spiritual Gifts. Chicago, Il.: Moody Press, 1975.

_____. Unwrap Your Spiritual Gifts. Wheaton, Il.: Victor Books, 1988.

Gee, Donald. Concerning Spiritual Gifts. Springfield, Mo.: Gospel Publishing House, 1972.

_____. Now That You've Been Baptized in the Spirit. Springfield, Mo.: Gospel Publishing House, 1972.

_____. Spiritual Gifts in the Work of the Ministry Today. Springfield, Mo.: Gospel Publishing House, 1963.

Geisler, Norman L., and Feinberg, Paul D. Introduction to Philosophy. Grand Rapids, Mi.: Baker Book House, 1988.

Gilquest, Peter E. Let's Quit Fighting About the Holy Spirit. Grand Rapids, Mi.: Zondervan Publishing House, 1974.

Gothard, Bill. How to Understand Spiritual Gifts. Oak Brook, Il.: Institute In Basic Life Principles, 1986.

Graham, Billy. The Holy Spirit. Waco, Tx.: Word Books Publisher, 1978.

Green, Michael. I Believe in the Holy Spirit. Grand Rapids, Mi.: Wm. B. Eerdmans Publishing Co., 1975.

Griffiths, Michael. Grace Gifts. Grand Rapids, Mi.: Wm. B. Eerdmans Publishing Co., 1979.

Grossman, Sigfried. There are Other Gifts than Tongues. Wheaton, Il.: Tyndale House Publishers, 1973.

Grudem, Wayne. The Gift of Prophecy in the New Testament and Today. Wheaton, Il.: Crossway Books, Good News Publishers, 1988.

Hall, Calvin S. and Nordby, Vernon J. A Primer of Jungian Psychology. New York and Scarborough, Ontario: A Mentor Book: New American Library, 1973.

Harbaugh, Gary L. God's Gifted People. Minneapolis, Mn.: Augsburg Publishing House, 1988.

Holdcroft, Thomas L. The Holy Spirit. Springfield, Mo.: Gospel Publishing House, 1979.

Horton, Harold. The Gifts of the Spirit. Springfield, Mo.: Gospel Publishing House, 1975.

Horton, Stanley M. What The Bible Says About The Holy Spirit. Springfield, Mo.: Gospel Publishing House, 1976.

_____., ed. Systematic Theology: A Pentecostal Perspective. Springfield, Mo.: Gospel Publishing House, 1994.

Hubbard, David Allen. Unwrapping Your Spiritual Gifts. Waco, Tx.: Word Books, 1985.

Jung, Carl G. Psychological Types. Princeton, N.J.: Princeton University Press, 1976

Keirsey, David; Bates, Marilyn. Please Understand Me Character & Temperament Types. Del Mar, Ca.: Prometheus Nemesis Book Company, 1984.

Kinghorn, Kenneth Cain. Gifts of the Spirit. Nashville, Tn.: Abingdon Press, 1976.

Lawrence, Gordon. People Types and Tiger Stripes. 2nd ed. Gainesville, Fl.: Center for Applications of Psychological Type, Inc., 1987.

MacGorman, Jack W. The Gifts of the Spirit. Nashville, Tn.: Broadman Press, 1974.

McRae, William J. The Dynamics of Spiritual Gifts. Grand Rapids, Mi.: Zondervan Publishing Co., 1976.

Muhlen, Heriburt. A Charismatic Theology. New York: Paulist Press, 1978.

Myers, Isabel Briggs, and McCaulley, Mary H. A Guide to the Development and Use of the Myers-Briggs Type Indicator. Palo Alto, Ca.: Consulting Psychologists Press, 1985.

Myers, Isabel Briggs, and Myers, Peter B. Gifts Differing. Palo Alto, Ca.: Consulting Psychologists Press Inc., 1980.

Newell, William R. Romans Verse by Verse. Chicago, Il.: Moody Press, 1982.

Packo, John E. Find & Use Your Spiritual Gifts. Camp Hill, Pa.: Christian Publications, 1986.

Pearlman, Myer. Knowing the Doctrines of the Bible. Springfield, Mo.: Gospel Publishing House, 1937.

Purkiser, W. T. The Gifts of the Spirit. Kansas City, Mo.: Beacon Hill Press, 1975.

Pytches, David. Spiritual Gifts in the Local Church. Minneapolis, Mn.: Bethany House Publishers, 1985.

Riggs, Ralph M. The Spirit Himself. Springfield, Mo.: Gospel Publishing House, 1949.

Stedman, Ray C. Body Life. Glendale, Ca.: Regal Books, 1972.

Thomas, Robert L. Understanding Spiritual Gifts. Chicago, Il.: Moody Press, 1978.

Torrey, R. A. The Baptism with the Holy Spirit. Minneapolis, Mn.: Bethany House Publishers, 1972.

Tuttle, Robert G., Jr. The Partakers. Nashville, Tn.: Abingdon, 1974.

Wagner, C. Peter. Your Spiritual Gifts Can Help Your Church Grow. Ventura, Ca.: Regal Books, 1979.

_____. ed. Signs and Wonders Today. Altamonte Springs, Fl.: Creation House Strang Communications Company, 1987.

Williams, Rodman J. Renewal Theology. Grand Rapids, Mi.: Zondervan Publishing Co., 1990.

Wimber, John. A Brief Sketch of Signs and Wonders Through the Church Age. Placentia, Ca.: Vineyard Christian Fellowship.

Yohn, Rick. Discover Your Spiritual Gift and Use It. Wheaton, Il.: Tyndale House Publishers, 1974.

_____. God's Holy Spirit for Christian Living. Irvine, Ca.: Harvest House Publishers, 1977.

Study Questions for

Chapter 1

Unraveling the Mystery of the
Motivational Gifts

1. Why is it vitally important for people to understand that the Motivational Gifts theory is not at odds with the traditional concept of the gifts of the Spirit?

2. Explain what the theory attempts to identify.

3. Does the concept of the prophet in this theory negate the traditional sense and understanding of the prophet as predictor and forthteller found elsewhere in the Bible?

4. Does the Motivational Gifts theory deny the function of the prophet (or the other gifts) in the traditional sense?

5. Why have some people summarily rejected the Motivational Gifts theory?

6. What is the traditional concept of the prophet?

7. Can you harmonize the concepts of the prophet in the traditional sense with the Motivational Gifts theory of the Prophet?

8. Is the Motivational Gifts theory given as an alternative to the traditional concept of the functions of these gifts?

9. Why are these particular gifts called Motivational Gifts?

10. Is truth learned through experience necessarily suspect just because it has come from experience?

Study Questions for

Chapter 2

Background to the Motivational Gifts

1. What is the first and primary thing that you must know and believe about spiritual gifts?

2. God has equipped each member of the Body of Christ with a special ability to do what He wants them to do. What is this "special ability" called?

3. What are the basic passages of Scripture that are pertinent to the understanding of spiritual gifts?

4. What are the three major lists of Gifts and how are they categorized?

5. Do you believe that God is the author (creator) of our personalities?

6. What does the phrase "All truth is God's truth" mean?

Study Questions for

Chapter 3

An Overview of the Motivational Gifts

1. What are the are seven Motivational Gifts?

2. It appears from the context of Romans 12 that these spiritual gifts are correlated with what?

3. How are the various members in the will of the head?

4. When people have a correct perspective of themselves (Rom 12:3) and their ministries, it follows that, in a general sense, they will naturally and automatically know what?

5. How are Christians like cinnamon and light?

6. Searching and knowing God's will involves service for God by properly evaluating what?

7. If your Motivational Gift is God's gift to you, what is your gift to Him?

8. Why is the term "Motivational" an accurate one for the function of these gifts?

9. What is another term that is also descriptive of the Motivational Gifts, and why?

10. What is one of the greatest keys to working as a "team"?

11. Why do some mature believers find it difficult to identify their primary gift?

12. What is a PAT-Mix?

Study Questions for

※※※※

Chapter 4

※※※※

Rose-Colored Glasses

1. How is it that our Motivational Gifts can be thought of as our "Rose-Colored Glasses"?

2. Discuss the various perspectives that might arise from each gift to a given circumstance or situation.

3. What is the danger in thinking that each person has only one primary Motivational Gift?

4. Explain the difference between what the author calls a "role" and a "gift."

Study Questions for

Chapter 5

Gift Projection

1. What is Gift Projection?

2. Have you ever projected your gift upon others?

3. Has anyone ever projected their gift upon you?

4. Since God is the Author of the Differences, how should we treat others with differing gifts?

5. Discuss David's refusal to wear Saul's armor and talk about how it relates to gift projection.

6. What is the falsification of giftedness?

7. Who besides parents are susceptible to the inclination of gift projection?

8. What is Gift Larceny?

Study Questions for

⌐⌐⌐⌐⌐⌐

Chapter 6

⌐⌐⌐⌐⌐⌐

Some Characteristic Traits of the Seven Motivational Gifts

1. How do we not confuse the gifts of Ephesians 4 and of 1 Corinthians 12 with the Motivational Gifts of Romans 12?

2. What does it mean when we say that a person has the Motivational Gift of Prophet?

3. Give at least one major characteristic of the Motivational Gift of Prophet (aka, Truth Teller).

4. Give at least one of the pitfalls for those with the Prophet Motivation.

5. Give at least one major characteristic of the Motivational Gift of Server.

6. Give at least one of the pitfalls for those with the Server Motivation.

7. Give at least one major characteristic of the Motivational Gift of Teacher.

8. Give at least one of the pitfalls for those with the Teacher Motivation.

9. Give at least one major characteristic of the Motivational Gift of Exhorter.

10. Give at least one of the pitfalls for those with the Exhorter Motivation.

11. Give at least one major characteristic of the Motivational Gift of Giver.

12. Give at least one of the pitfalls for those with the Giver Motivation.

13. Give at least one major characteristic of the Motivational Gift of Administrator.

14. Give at least one of the pitfalls for those with the Administrator Motivation.

15. Give at least one major characteristic of the Motivational Gift of Mercy.

16. Give at least one of the pitfalls for those with the Mercy Motivation.

Study Questions for

Chapter 7

Biblical Personality Examples of the Seven Motivational Gifts

1. What were the two main things that the Apostle Paul did when he learned that Peter had gotten himself sidetracked from the gospel of grace?

2. People with the Motivation of Prophet will speak the truth in the face of what?

3. Did Jesus tell Martha to stop doing what she was doing and join with Mary in sitting at his feet? Why or why not?

4. Name the three traits of the Motivational Gift of Teacher in Apollos.

5. Name the three traits of the Motivational Gift of Teacher in Luke.

6. What did the apostles nickname Joseph, and why?

7. Who was right about John Mark, the Apostle Paul or Barnabas?

8. What is found in the words "you sent a gift more than once for my needs"?

9. How is the Widow of Zarephath a picture of Christians who don't know what their gifts are?

10. Administrators are good at defining what?

11. One of the main motivations of the Administrator is what?

12. The person with the Mercy Motivation will be able to identify with and actually feel what?

Study Questions for

Chapter 8

The Motivational Gifts in Ministry

1. What is the implication in the words *charisma* and *chara*.

2. Why are some pastors burned-out and exhibit no joy in their ministries?

3. Do only Christians have these gifts?

4. Does the position of the innate quality of the Motivational Gifts imply that these gifts are anything less than supernatural?

5. It is important to point out that neither the _____ of the Spirit (1 Corinthians 12) nor the _____ gifts (Ephesians 4:11) are inherent gifts.

6. Even though non-Christians have these inherent Motivational Gifts, how are the gifts properly exercised?

7. To the extent that a single Christian is not functioning in his or her gift, to that degree what is weakened?

8. How can pastors have the greatest effectiveness with the least amount of weariness?

9. Many larger churches have attempted to remedy the burnout problem by having several pastors on staff. How can a knowledge of the Motivational Gifts help in this task?

10. What would be a dynamic ministry context?

11. What is a common mistake that laypeople make in their thinking, and how can this be corrected?

Study Questions for

Chapter 9

Do Opposites Attract?
A Prevailing Myth in Our Culture

1. Is the old saying that "opposites attract" always true, often true, seldom true, never true?

2. Statistically, are people who are the same (or similar) attracted to each other more often or less often than those who are opposites?

3. How does a Motivational-Gifts knowledge help in counseling?

4. What is the story of Pygmalion in Greek mythology, and how does it relate to married couples today?

5. Why is there the need for a proper understanding of the Motivational Gifts among couples?

Study Questions for

Chapter 10

The Walston Gifts Indicator
Determining Your Motivational Gifts

1. What is the *Walston Gifts Indicator*?

2. Why must one take great care in "identifying" a child's personality type?

3. What is your PAT-Mix?

Study Questions for

⌒ↂↀↂ⌒

Appendix A

⌒ↂↀↂ⌒

A Review of the Historical Development of the Motivational Gifts Theory

1. Does the theory of the Motivational Gifts claim that some gifts are supernatural and some are natural?

2. Does the human exercise of the Motivational Gifts suggest that the "personality-types theory" must lead to an anti-supernaturalistic interpretation of Romans 12:6-8?

3. Are non-Christians a part of God's creation?

4. What is the author's purpose in using Psalm 139:13-16?

5. In the Motivational-Gifts theory, the _____ of the gift is described. This description of the _____ of the gift rather than the gift itself cannot be done when the _____ of the Spirit are the topic. For example, one cannot simply identify a tongues-gifted individual from the

perspective of _____ characteristics.

6. How is it evident that one has mixed the gifts categories?

Study Questions for

Appendix B

A Brief Theology of Spiritual Gifts

1. What are the three major lists of gifts?

2. What is the significance of the author pointing out that in Ephesians 4, it is the gift of apostle, not *apostleship*, prophet not *prophecy*, evangelist not *evangelism*, and pastors and teachers not *pastoring* and *teaching*?

3. How many "Offices" are there in the Church, and what are they?

4. Is Ephesians 4:11 emphasizing office designations?

5. Is the term "office" an appropriate label for the five

gifts listed in Ephesians 4:11?

6. Can an "office" or an "intangible gift" teach and prepare others for the work of the ministry?

7. What are the two sub-categories within the Ministry Gifts?

8. What gifts are listed under each sub-category?

9. What are the three sub-categories within the Manifestations?

10. What are the gifts listed under each sub-category?

11. List the seven gifts under Category Three, i.e., the Motivational Gifts.

12. Under Category One, define Apostles.

13. Under Category One, define Prophets.

14. Under Category One, define Evangelists.

15. Under Category One, define Pastors.

16. Under Category One, define Teachers.

17. Under Category Two, define Word of Wisdom.

18. Under Category Two, define Word of Knowledge.

19. Under Category Two, define Discerning of Spirits.

20. Under Category Two, define Faith.

21. Under Category Two, define Workings of Miracles.

22. Under Category Two, define Gifts of Healings.

23. Under Category Two, define Prophecy.

24. Under Category Two, define Tongues.

25. Under Category Two, define Interpretation of Tongues.

26. Under Category Three, define Prophet.

27. Under Category Three, define Server.

28. Under Category Three, define Teacher.

29. Under Category Three, define Exhorter.

30. Under Category Three, define Giver.

31. Under Category Three, define Administrator.

32. Under Category Three, define Mercy.

Printed in the United States
97864LV00003B/92/A

9 781591 602229